Born Again . . .
in Medjugorje

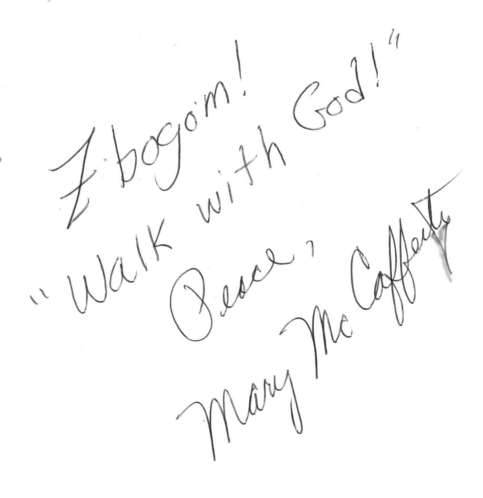

Zbogom!

"Walk with God!"

Peace,

Mary Mc Cafferty

Born Again . . .
in Medjugorje

A Memoir

by Mary Hendel McCafferty

Cover photo by the author
Internal photos by the author or her mother, Mary Hendel

A publication of Not Forgotten Publishing Services
Editing, production, and layout by Alice S. Morrow Rowan
NotForgottenPublishing@gmail.com

Printed in the United States of America

This book is dedicated to my mom,
Mary Bernadette (Carr) Hendel

It is filled with memories from our first pilgrimage together to Medjugorje, and includes memories from my childhood that led to this time in my life. Being with my mother in Medjugorje was one of the greatest gifts God has given me and writing this memoir has allowed me to live it all over again.

Mom, although the memories shared here are mine, you were by my side every step of the way and I am so grateful for that gift. It was life-changing for me. I am so thankful for all of the times we've traveled to Medjugorje together, beginning each trip with a Bailey's Irish Cream. I hope that you too will relive Medjugorje while reading this memoir.

As we prepared to leave on our first pilgrimage, we had no idea what we were about to experience.

2-4-6 Mary

CONTENTS

EPILOGUE

APPENDIXES

"A Pharisee in the Sanhedrin named Gamaliel, a teacher of the law, respected by all the people, stood up, ordered the Apostles to be put outside for a short time, and said to the Sanhedrin, 'Fellow children of Israel, be careful what you are about to do to these men. Some time ago, Theudas appeared, claiming to be someone important, and about four hundred men joined him, but he was killed, and all those who were loyal to him were disbanded and came to nothing. After him came Judas the Galilean at the time of the census. He also drew people after him, but he too perished and all who were loyal to him were scattered. So now I tell you, have nothing to do with these men, and let them go. For if this endeavor or this activity is of human origin, it will destroy itself. But if it comes from God, you will not be able to destroy them; you may even find yourselves fighting against God.' They were persuaded by him. After recalling the Apostles, they had them flogged, ordered them to stop speaking in the name of Jesus, and dismissed them. So they left the presence of the Sanhedrin, rejoicing that they had been found worthy to suffer dishonor for the sake of the name. And all day long, both at the temple and in their homes, they did not stop teaching and proclaiming the Christ, Jesus. In the same way, I desire to say, if this endeavor or this activity is of human origin, it will destroy itself. But if it comes from God, you will not be able to destroy them; you may even find yourselves fighting against God."

Acts 5:34–42

Chapter One

IN THE BEGINNING

Maureen and Fred . . . and how it all began

It all began when my high school friend Maureen (Thompson) Lomady and her husband, Fred, whom we hadn't seen in several years, came to our home in Mt. Holly, New Jersey. At the time, Joey and I had two young children, Matthew and Emily, ages two and a half and one. I knew our friends had recently gone to Europe but had no idea that the question, "So, how was your trip?" was about to change my life. On that afternoon visit, they shared with us about the apparitions taking place in Medjugorje, a village located in Bosnia-Herzegovina. Apparently, in June of 1981, six children—four girls and two boys ages ten to sixteen—began experiencing visions of the Blessed Virgin Mary, the mother of Jesus, on a daily basis. These six—Ivanka Ivankovic, Mirjana Dragicevic, Vicka Ivankovic, Ivan Dragicevic, Marija Pavlovic, and Jakov Colo—are now referred to as "visionaries" (see Appendix A for brief bios).

We hadn't heard of this before and it was now 1987. At the time, we weren't practicing our faith very seriously and attending Sunday Mass was not a priority for us, but how could this be? Six years, every day, and we're just hearing about it now?

Why I believed immediately I'll never know; but I will be forever grateful for the gift of faith I received that day. I suppose I could say it's partly because Maureen, whom I had known since high school and who had been a typical teenager in the 1970s, had obviously been transformed by these events. She and Fred had gone to Medjugorje and expressed no doubt about the authenticity of the apparitions as they relayed the details to us. Maureen never said "supposed" apparitions; she spoke matter-of-factly, giving the details as she believed them to be true.

I have since experienced many reactions when I've shared this story with others—from immediate belief to complete skepticism. All I know is, when Maureen and Fred finished sharing with us that day, I felt my life was about to change. I was experiencing God's love in a new way. My heart pounded as they spoke and I had goose bumps as I heard Mary's messages of "peace, prayer, fasting, conversion, reconciliation and strong faith." One of her first messages in the early days was, "I have come to tell the world that God exists." She also said, "Peace, peace, and only peace must reign between God and man and among humankind."

Maureen then told me that she planned to return to Medjugorje later that year and invited me to join her. The fact that I had never traveled anywhere of great distance without Joey prompted my immediate reply, "I don't think I could *ever* go that far—especially with two young children at home!"

More About the Author . . . before going forward, let's go back

The following is taken from a talk I have given in recent years while on retreat with the high school juniors and seniors from my church, St. John Neumann, in Lancaster, Pennsylvania. It gives a glimpse into my life in "1987 B.C.," that is, Before Conversion.

I grew up in an Irish Catholic family with five brothers and four sisters in a humble Cape Cod style home in Ardsley, Pennsylvania. Every one of us went to Catholic school from grades 1 to 12. We attended church every Sunday and Holy Day. The fact that our backyard ended at Queen of Peace Church's parking lot made it impossible for us to miss Sunday Mass—no matter what the weather! We learned to pray the rosary because my parents insisted we pray it every night in May and October, which are the months dedicated to Mary, so I was very familiar with the prayer. I thought of using the words "invited us to pray" but that wouldn't have been accurate. My parents insisted we pray the rosary. With our plastic beads in hand, we would all kneel around my parents' bed. My mother would place the ivory-colored statue of Mary with the round wooden base at the head of the bed, between the pillows. I remember my mother being very serious about praying the rosary. As we took turns leading the prayers, my youngest sister, Terry, would often begin the Hail Mary with the wrong words and the rest of us would laugh. My mother would say, "If you were thinking about your prayers, you wouldn't be laughing." I can still remember my dad, who was known as the strict one of the two, trying to hide the smile on his face. Sometimes Moms just have to be the bad guy!

I remember myself as a young child saying my nighttime prayers before bed with my sisters. There was such comfort having them with me as we knelt before the crucifix in our room. As we grew older, one by one our little group dwindled down to where I remember each of us saying our prayers alone. As time went by, I stopped praying before bed altogether. When I was young I had a desire to talk to God; as the years passed, those talks became less and less frequent.

I can remember that when I was in the seventh grade I wished that I was more popular. I had a few good friends, but I wasn't considered popular. In a class of eighty students, I wasn't invited to a single party that year. I was desperate to be liked by the others. I decided that summer that upon entering the eighth grade I was going to change . . . and I did. I became the joke teller. As a matter of fact, I became fairly good at it! I remember feeling that year was a good year. I made lots of friends and was invited to every party. I enjoyed making people laugh and I really enjoyed having more friends.

When I entered high school, the trend continued, but just like my own personality, the personality of my jokes had changed. They went from being really funny to really crude, and as I became more accepted by others, God was less welcome in my own life. Several years passed and I thought I was happy. I had a lot of friends. By the time I left high school, the only time I gave to God was at Mass on Sundays and that's only because it was the rule in our home. God was in my head but no longer in my heart.

Has anyone ever said anything to you that you know you will never, ever forget? Something that wasn't intended to hurt you when they said it but it struck you like a lightning bolt? That happened to me when I was about twenty-one years old. I was out one night with some friends and one of my older brothers was there. We were all sitting around having a good time and someone was asked to tell a joke they had recently heard. The person declined, saying, "It was too gross to tell." My brother then said something that I will never, ever forget. He confidently spoke up and said, "Mary will tell it. She's a pig!"

Those words struck my heart like nothing I had ever felt before. I had always enjoyed making people laugh, but I never thought that people thought of me in that way. There we were, having a good time, and all of a sudden I felt like every eye in the room was looking at me, just waiting for me to perform in my usual manner. I couldn't do it. The lump in my throat was so hard, the pain I felt was like I had swallowed something and was going to choke. However, crying was definitely out of the question. There was a lot of prodding and encouraging going on for me to tell the joke, but I knew I couldn't. All of a sudden I felt like a little child again and I didn't know where to turn. When my brother noticed the look on my face, he came over, put his arm around me, and just sat there silently. He didn't know what to say. He had no idea what was going on but he knew something had just happened.

The seeds for change had been planted that night . . . but sometimes seeds take a long time to sprout.

Several years passed and I was now married with two children. Although I had changed somewhat, I had not yet invited God back into my life. The night that everything really changed for me was the night my very good friend from high school, Maureen, came to visit with her husband, Fred. We hadn't seen each other for several years.

I can only tell you a little bit about me and Maureen. We aren't proud of the choices we made in high school. We weren't really that bad; indeed, at the time we didn't think of ourselves as bad at all, but God certainly had no say in the decisions we were making. Some of those decisions involved drinking alcohol, and with that came more bad decisions. I know now that if I had let God in, I would have done things much differently.

Now, years later, Maureen and her husband had come to visit us. As we sat around the kitchen table, the conversation turned to Maureen. She started telling us how she had allowed God back into her life. The way it happened and the story she told had me in tears over and over again. Here she was, telling me how God's love had changed her life. For the first time in my life I was actually talking with a friend about God and it wasn't uncomfortable; it was, however, physically and emotionally draining.

I cried that night because I saw such joy in my friend's face as she shared about God's forgiveness. I saw something new in her eyes that I had not seen there before. It was a peace that had not been there in high *school. The fun and mischievous twinkle in her eyes that she had always had as a teen was still there—but now it was different. It was pure, and it was opening my own heart that had been closed for so long.*

We sat and talked that night for hours. Maureen and Fred did most of the talking; I did most of the crying, but it was a good cry. Those were tears of cleansing. The best part was that Maureen cried with me. She cried because she knew the love that she had accepted from God was being passed on to me and now I was accepting His love.

When Maureen and Fred left our home that night, the seeds of change planted so many years before by my brother's unexpected words began to take root. I was speechless as I sat in my living room. I was exhausted emotionally. I felt as though someone had come through my house and taken every piece of furniture and turned it upside down. My life was upside down, but it was okay. It was time for a change!

The next morning was Sunday. I hadn't been attending Mass on a regular basis and when I did go it was out of habit or guilt, but this day I couldn't wait to be in church. I couldn't wait to be there before God to thank Him. I felt like a child again. I could not stop the tears as they flowed from deep within my heart. These were not tears of shame; they were tears of joy and thanksgiving. I thanked God for many reasons that day, but more than anything else I thanked Him for waiting for me. He knew I would come back and He never gave up on me. I have learned since then that I don't have to wait for Sunday Mass to talk to God. He is and always has been right beside me no matter where I am. He is always there for me.

After sharing my story with the retreatants, I showed them three clips from the "Jesus of Nazareth" movie; specifically, the stories of Peter's denial and Judas's betrayal, and the parable of the Rich Young Man. Then I went on to say:

If I were asked to compare myself to Peter, Judas, and the Rich Young Man, I would say I was most like Peter. I too denied Jesus. I denied knowing Him by my words and actions that indicated, "I don't know you and I don't need you in my life." Peter denied Jesus three times, but I denied Him many more. However, Jesus waited. He waited patiently, and all that time He loved me. When I was in grade school, Jesus felt my loneliness. He cried tears of sadness for me the night my brother

*unknowingly uttered those hurtful yet profound words. As I felt the
pain in my heart, Jesus felt that pain too because, as I know now, He is
inside of me. In everything that has happened to me in my life, He has
been there with me.*

*Now, years later, He cried tears of joy for me as He watched my
heart open up to His love. And when I returned to His Church on that
very special Sunday, I know He was smiling at me. It was as if I could feel
Him wrapping His loving arms around me as He allowed me to weep
gently in His loving embrace. I knew that day that I was Home to stay.*

We Heard the Call . . . and we answered

After Maureen and Fred's visit, over the next few years I watched many
tapes and read every book I could on the events in Medjugorje. I had
such a desire to know more. I gave birth to our third child, Patrick, on
December 12, 1988 (the feast of Our Lady of Guadalupe). As time
passed, I knew I was being called to Medjugorje. My desire to go
where Our Lady was appearing was so strong. After talking to Mom,
we agreed we both wanted to go there and we came up with a plan.
She would ask Joey for me and I would ask Dad for her. They both said
yes and that was that!

Maureen's recommendation to travel to Medjugorje with Helen
Sarcevic, who lives in Clarks Summit, Pennsylvania, turned out to be a
gift in itself. Helen's family is Croatian, she speaks the language, and as
we later found out, she knows the visionaries personally.

Strange Happenings . . . but don't be discouraged

Maureen warned me that whenever she planned a trip to Medjugorje,
"strange" things would suddenly occur to make her wonder whether
she should be going or not. One of her pilgrimages was in 1986 and
during the planning stages of her trip, on April 26, 1986, the Chernobyl
nuclear accident took place in the Ukraine. As would be expected,
travelers were canceling their plans and not flying anywhere in that
direction. Maureen and her group, however, were not discouraged.
She told us that the seventy-two pilgrims (people who go on a journey

for religious reasons) were the only passengers on their very large airplane crossing the Atlantic Ocean to Europe. I remember her telling me with a smile, "At one point the pilot came back to see this crazy group of people who weren't deterred by a nuclear disaster."

Warning: Travel Advisory . . . do we cancel?

At Maureen's recommendation, Mom and I made our plans to travel with Helen Sarcevic and MIR-Peace. MIR-Peace is the name the Sarcevic family has chosen for the retreat pilgrimages they offer to Medjugorje pilgrims. We sent in our $200 deposit. The nine-day trip would cost us $980 each, including airfare and ground transportation, two full meals a day, and overnight accommodations in one of the villagers' homes. In the summer, as our November trip approached, the newspapers began warning of a "travel advisory" to certain parts of Europe—namely Yugoslavia—due to political unrest. Of course this did not sit well with Joey, so I called the European Embassy to decide if we should cancel our trip. I was told that it was safe to travel along the route we intended, so on November 13, 1990, we were on our way to experience heaven on earth.

Chapter Two

TUESDAY, November 13, 1990

✦

Medjugorje . . . here we come!

I remember it as though it were yesterday. Dad drove Mom to my in-law's house on Fulmer Street in Philadelphia, where Joey and I joined them with our three children. We had arranged for an airport van to pick us up at this location because it was the midway point between Ardsley and Mt. Holly. I was thirty-one years old, had never been out of the country, had certainly never left my husband and children for nine days—heck, I had never even driven to the New Jersey shore—and there we were, heading to Yugoslavia! What was I thinking? What in the world made me think I could ever do this?

The driver waited as we said our good-byes, which were prolonged by anxious hugs. I'll always remember something Joey's mother did after she hugged me. With her right thumb, she made the sign of the cross on my forehead. It was something no one, other than a priest, had ever done and it tugged at my heart in an unexpected way. She will never know how much that one small gesture meant to me. After my pilgrimage, I began blessing my husband and children with the sign of the cross whenever we parted.

As we seated ourselves in the van and waved out the window to Joey and the kids, a terrible reality set in: they can't see me! I hadn't noticed before we got in that the windows were tinted. I could see my children standing on the curbside grass, questioning, looking for me, saying "Where is she?" "Where's Mommy?" "I can't see her!" As the driver pulled away, I was in tears because I had left my whole family behind and they didn't even see me wave good-bye. For those who don't think this is a big deal, let me tell you: it's a Hendel tradition to wave from the car whenever you're saying good-bye. Whenever we visit Mom and Dad, no matter how long the day has been, Mom, and often Dad, always stands on the front porch waving as we pull away. The doubts began to set in . . . but not for long.

Helen had asked us to arrive at Kennedy Airport in New York three hours prior to departure. She had told us to look for the MIR-Peace sign in the ticket area and, sure enough, as soon as we stepped through the doorway with our bags, there she stood with her sign and a smile. We learned that *mir* is the Croatian word for *peace.*

Our group of forty-seven pilgrims introduced ourselves to one another. The priest traveling with us was Fr. Walter Sempko from Harrisburg and he was going to be celebrating Mass right there at the airport before we took off . . . a whole new experience for me! Fr. Sempko was a friendly priest and, after a brief conversation, he asked me, "Do you like to sing?" I said yes, and to that he replied, "Great! Then you can lead us during the Mass!" I quickly declined the offer, saying, "I only sing in the shower." What a dumb thing to say to a priest! At least it got me out of singing in front of everyone.

As it turned out, there were many women with the name *Mary* in our group of forty-seven. I don't know if being named Mary is a prerequisite for an invite to Medjugorje, but I figured that with my husband's name being Joseph I was definitely a shoe-in! We later realized that five of the Marys would be staying in the same house, including me and Mom. Someone mentioned that this situation might get confusing and Fr. Sempko, who had heard that I had three children ages "almost 2, 4, and almost 6," decided to call me "2-4-6 Mary."

As our plane lifted off, it was hard to believe we were on our way to Medjugorje. After reading books and seeing videos of the events going on there, I had become quite familiar with each visionary. I had seen videos of the children during apparitions and had no doubt that they were authentic. I knew each of their names and the names of some of the priests in the parish. I had read about the huge cross on Mt. Krizevac, also known as Cross Mountain, and about Apparition Hill, where Our Lady had first appeared to the children. Yes, we were really on our way.

Excerpts from the Journal I Kept on This Pilgrimage

"It's 7:09 P.M. and our plane is getting ready for take-off. The first flight to Geneva will take 6½ hours. I know Joey and the kids are thinking of me at this moment."

"Take-off was fine and now we're on our way. We are sitting next to Joe McCormick, a youth group leader. We told him where we are from and he told us he goes on rescue missions at abortion clinics in the Glenside area, right next to where I grew up. As it turns out, he knows Maureen and Fred Lomady very well! What a small world!"

"We arrived in Geneva at 8:00 A.M. for a layover of about one hour. We are now on our way to Zurich. It's 9:30 A.M. here and it's 3:30 A.M. at home. Joey and the kids are sound asleep in our dimly lit home; I'm in Switzerland on my way to Medjugorje."

"Our third leg of the trip was from Zurich to Zagreb. While we were in the airport in Zagreb, we were getting to know Janet and Mary (two sisters in their early 20s). Janet told us that she and Mary were going to be staying in the home of Ivanka— one of the Medjugorje visionaries! My heart immediately sank, wishing we were also going to be staying there. Susan Minnick, another pilgrim, came to me and said that Mom and I were also going to be staying the week with Ivanka!! This is our first blessing in Medjugorje!"

Praying the Rosary . . . Nan's rosary?

I'd begun using a blue crystal beaded rosary for prayer in the weeks leading up to our departure. I had to reacquaint myself with this prayer because I had not prayed it since I was a child. Because of the May processions at Queen of Peace School and growing up with the family tradition of praying the rosary every night in May and October, I was able to make my way through it. I also have childhood memories of returning from school to find Nan, my grandmother on my mom's side, visiting. If she was sitting in the chair in the living room, whether awake or asleep, she always had her rosary beads in her hand. When she was up and about, if they were not in her hand, they were in her housecoat pocket.

I'd never known anyone who prayed the rosary more than Nan. I had decided that this prayer would be a good way to prepare for my pilgrimage. I often thought of Nan as I used these blue crystal beads and considered that they could possibly have been hers. Nan had died several years before this trip, in January of 1987, so praying the rosary now just brought me a little closer to her. After she died I had prayed for a very long time that God had taken her to heaven.

Being immature in my faith and new to all of the miraculous events of Medjugorje, I was hoping, I have to admit, for a miracle of my own. To see the sun spin and throw off color as described in books, or to have the links of my rosary turn from silver to gold as I had heard happened to others would be sure proof that these events were real. Although I really did believe in my heart that Mary was appearing there, I was hoping for one of these signs and would often peek at my rosary to see if anything had begun to happen to it—and this was before we had even left New Jersey!

Nan Planted the Seed of Faith . . . through her own story

Although I doubt Nan ever knew it, she had a strong influence on me by planting a seed that opened my heart to the question, "Is there really a heaven?" She told me the following story sometime after her son, my Uncle Don, died unexpectedly at the age of forty-one, when I was in the seventh grade.

Nan had been so overwhelmed when Don died that she had cried for a very long time. She couldn't seem to move beyond her grief and one day she promised God that if He would just give her a sign that Don was with Him, she would not grieve anymore.

One night as she was lying awake, she suddenly became aware that Don was there in the room with her, standing at the foot of her bed. He was wearing a brown hooded robe with the kind of rope belt that the Franciscans wear. He looked at her and smiled. I remember her saying he didn't say anything to her, but his smile and his eyes told her, "I'm OK." She said she knew he didn't want her to cry over him anymore.

Anyone who had ever met Nan would have to agree that she was not prone to making up stories. However, Nan told me she had stopped sharing this story with most people because at one point one of her family members hadn't believed her and had said, "You were just dreaming." She told me it was not a dream and that it was as real to her as anything had ever been, but because there were those who didn't believe, she had stopped telling the story. For some reason she was prompted to tell it to me.

I don't know why she told me this story or how many had heard it before me, but Mom and I discussed this topic on one occasion. Our memories were similar except that Mom remembers Nan saying she heard him "say" he was OK and I remember Nan saying she "knew" he was OK. The point is, because Nan shared this story with me, I had a reason to believe that Uncle Don was in heaven. It said to me, "heaven must be real."

Chapter Three

WEDNESDAY, November 14, 1990

Ivanka, Our Hostess with the Warm Smile . . . there to serve

Eventually, after twenty-four hours, having taken three flights with delays in between and a three-hour bus ride along the beautiful Adriatic Coast, at 11:30 P.M. on Wednesday we arrived on the doorstep of our hostess, Ivanka Ivankovic Elez, one of the six Medjugorje visionaries. I had seen her picture in books and videos, but my heart skipped a beat when I came face to face with this visionary and was immediately touched by her warm smile. Little did I know that one day, eighteen years later, I would have the privilege of hosting this beautiful young lady in my own home in Lancaster, Pennsylvania.

Our large group was divided into smaller groups that stayed in three homes in the village. We had twenty-one in our group. Mary Pinto and her five-year-old son, Stephen Felgendreger, were two of the pilgrims we stayed with at Ivanka's home. Mary and Stephen were in Medjugorje hoping for a miracle. Mary shared that one day five months earlier she had noticed Stephen's eyes beginning to cross. Her doctor performed normal finger-to-nose tests with him and immediately sent him to a neurologist. An MRI discovered that he had an inoperable brain tumor. By the time we met Stephen he had already been through six weeks of daily chemotherapy and had lost his hair. Mary had traveled all the way to Medjugorje in the hope of receiving a healing for her son.

Ivanka humbly greeted us at her front door in her bathrobe. After all, it was 11:30 at night. I realized right then that she was not there to impress us, she was there to serve. Waiting for us was a meal of stuffed peppers, mashed potatoes, soup, and bread. Ivanka knew that, after our long journey, we were tired and hungry. When the meal was over, she insisted we leave the dishes for her and that we get a good night's sleep. We could help on other days, but this night we would rest.

We heard that Ivanka had delivered her second child, Josef, just five months earlier. It turned out that his birthdate, June 14, was the exact date that Stephen had been diagnosed with his brain tumor. Mary, in all of her exhaustion, found comfort in that little coincidence.

Stephen Felgendreger . . . our own little angel

Stephen was a sweet little boy with the most pleasant smile and personality. He never complained the entire trip and was such a joy to have around. His mother said he never cried during any of his chemo treatments and only flinched when he got his needles. The right side of his body had little mobility (he had difficulty moving both his arm and his leg). As a result, Mary carried him almost everywhere. Mary's sister, Margaret, accompanied her on the trip to help take care of Stephen. A wonderful memory I have of Stephen is teaching him a joke, which he then told over the microphone on the bus during our travels. I had asked him, "What did the painter say to the wall?" The answer: "One more crack and I'll plaster ya!" Stephen loved to tell that joke and was overheard more than once retelling it. Another sweet thing about Stephen was his love for Jesus and Mary. Whenever we passed a statue of Jesus or Mary, he would wave and say hello to them as only a child could do.

Chapter Four

THURSDAY, November 15, 1990

St. James Church . . . even more beautiful in real life

We woke up Thursday morning refreshed and excited to begin our first full day in Medjugorje. After a simple breakfast of homemade breads, cheese, orange juice, and coffee, we took the twenty-minute walk through the tobacco fields and vineyards—the main crops of Medjugorje's farmers—to St. James Church. Although a cab was always available, we came to enjoy this peaceful walk throughout the week. As we rounded the final bend in the road, I could see the twin steeples of St. James Church straight ahead. I had seen pictures of this church many times over the past few years, but seeing it for the first time in real life caused my heart to skip a beat. It was so beautiful against the clear morning sky and it appeared much larger than I had expected. In the background was Cross Mountain, or Mt. Krizevac. We could just barely make out the cross at the top—a cross that I had read was thirty-six feet high!

The Sun Is Spinning . . . but don't look!

As we arrived, the German Mass was still taking place inside the church, so we waited outside for the English Mass to begin. Groups of pilgrims from Ireland, America, and other English-speaking countries were gathering with us. I was having a conversation with Fr. Sempko when a bit of commotion coming from our new friends caught my attention. They were calling my name and shouting, "Mary! Mary! Look at the sun!" Without hesitation Fr. Sempko said, "Don't look at it."

As I've already admitted, I had started looking at the links on my rosary to see if they had changed color even before we had arrived in Medjugorje! So, you can imagine how it felt to be told, "Don't look."

I did the respectful thing and continued my conversation with Fr. Sempko, but as we talked the group continued calling, "Mary, Mary! Look at the sun!" Their insistent cries were getting my attention. Tapping his fingers to his heart, Fr. Sempko said, "It's what happens in here that matters the most."

I couldn't stand it any longer and replied, "But Father, I *really* want to look!"

He calmly said, "It's up to you."

Of course I quickly turned to look at the sun, expecting to see what the others were seeing, but I was disappointed and had to turn away immediately. I saw nothing except the same blinding sun I see every day. I was not able to look directly at it, and when I looked back at my friends they were staring at the sun and experiencing something that was not meant for me.

Mass for English-Speaking Pilgrims . . . a whole new experience

That morning I experienced the Mass like never before. From 7:30 A.M. to 1:00 P.M. every day, Mass is celebrated hour after hour, in one language and then another. Monday through Saturday, the 7:30 A.M. Mass is in Croatian for the people of St. James parish, then at 9:00 in German, 10:00 in English, 11:00 in Italian, and so on. Crowds would gather outside the church waiting for the previous Mass to finish. Whenever there were pilgrims of more languages than time allowed for Mass inside the church, such as Polish, Korean and others, Masses were said in the "Yellow Building," which sits adjacent to St. James Church and is used for large gatherings. It is announced ahead of time when one of the visionaries, a priest of the parish, or another guest will be giving a talk in this building.

When it was time for our Mass and the German-speaking pilgrims were exiting, there was a sudden rush of English-speaking pilgrims trying to get into the church. I had never seen anything like it. The church filled up quickly with people from America, Ireland, England, Australia, South Africa, and many other English-speaking countries. As soon as the pews in the church were filled, the next unusual occurrence began. People didn't stand at the back of the church as they do at home. Instead, they came to the front of the church and sat right on the steps of the altar. Then they continued to fill up the floor space—right down the aisles from the front to the back of the church. Even the extra seats in the choir loft were taken by pilgrims, and all of this happened in a matter of minutes. This, remember, was a Thursday morning—not a Sunday. This was *daily* Mass at St. James Church in Medjugorje, as we would come to experience it, six days of the week! Sunday had another busy schedule. And I've yet to describe the International Mass that takes place every evening for *all* of the pilgrims!

The music was beautiful, but it was not the music of the choir that I am remembering—it is the voices of all of the pilgrims. Everyone sang with hearts so filled with joy and happiness that I was immediately brought to tears. If there was a choir leading that day, you wouldn't have known it, because every voice in the church was lifted up in song, drowning out anyone's chance to stand out.

At that first morning Mass, the words of the Gospel came alive for me. It was as if I was hearing them for the first time and my heart pounded as the words were spoken. I cannot remember the priest's homily specifically, but what I do remember is that several times as he spoke, the pilgrims broke into applause—definitely another first!

At that Holy Mass I seemed to experience heaven on earth. What I didn't realize at the time was that I had been given this gift my whole life, at every Mass.

Mary's Camera . . . her joy was short-lived

After the Mass was finished, our group gathered outside to go over the plans for the day. Mary Pinto came from the church and was obviously upset. She said she was with Stephen at the Mass and when it was finished she went to gather her things and her camera was gone. It had been right there on the pew with her and someone had definitely taken it. She was so frustrated and said, "I liked this place better when I was at home!" She said she didn't belong there. Helen very calmly told her, "We will find it. Let's ask Our Lady to help us get it back." That was not the last time we would hear Helen sincerely express this kind of confidence in Our Lady.

The Club House . . . Slavica

After the Mass we went to the Clubhouse, as Helen called it, for our first of many visits. The Clubhouse is located just a short walk from the church. It is the home of Helen's good friend Sima Vasilj. A third of our group was staying there that week. Because of it's convenient location, just a short walk beyond the Yellow Building, the Mir-Peace groups meet there throughout the week to go over the day's happenings and to hear what will take place the following day. Almost every night during our stay, after the activities at the church, our group would go to the Clubhouse for a cup of coffee or a glass of homemade wine, crackers and cheese, homemade breads, and Croatian cookies. It was always a great place to relax, hear what others in the group had experienced during the day, and get to know everyone better.

This particular morning we had a special visitor at the Clubhouse. Her name was Slavica. This young girl was part of a prayer group that had been formed at Our Lady's request. She told us that Our Lady, through the "inner locutionists"[1] Jelena Vasilj and Marijana Vasilj, had invited the young people of the parish to begin a prayer group. She had asked them to commit three hours a day to prayer. She'd asked those in the group to wait three years before considering marriage or a vocation, in order to determine what God was calling them to do with their lives.

Slavica said, "Our Lady wants us to go home and *live* the messages of peace, prayer, fasting, and conversion and to live our own lives as an example for others so that they too can hear and desire to live the messages." She told us, "Our Lady also wants to thank all of those who have gone home and started prayer groups." The last thing she said was that Our Lady would be appearing to the visionaries on Friday night at 10:00 on Cross Mountain and that she invited us there to pray for peace.

---

[1] The inner locutionists have said they hear messages within their heart and see Mary with the eyes of their heart—which is different from the three-dimensional vision of the Blessed Virgin that the others see during their apparitions. Jelena and Marijana had begun receiving their messages in 1982 and 1983, respectively.

The International Mass at St. James Church . . . we are one

In the early years of the apparitions Our Lady suggested that all of those who came to Medjugorje should celebrate the Mass together— to be together as one. At one point the children asked Our Lady, "Should the people come to you or should they go to the church?" Our Lady responded, "If you have a choice either to come to me or to go to the Holy Mass, no, don't come to me. Go to the Holy Mass, because that is where you will find my Son."

The evening Mass is prayed in Croatian because that is the language of the parish; however, as more people came from foreign countries it became difficult for many to follow the Mass. Although the pilgrims did come together in the evening, they also began requesting to have Masses said in their own languages in the morning. Now pilgrims often attend both Masses.

Each evening, one hour before the Holy Mass, the rosary is prayed. The beginning of each prayer (the Our Father, Hail Mary, and Glory Be) is prayed in the Croatian language and then the second half of each prayer is prayed simultaneously in all of the languages of those present. Verses of "Ave Maria" are sung between each decade. It is a beautiful way for the people of the world to pray as one. For years now, at 5:40 each evening (at 6:40 during certain times of the year), Our Lady has appeared to the children. At that exact time during the rosary, there is a moment of silence and all become aware that this is the moment when Our Lady is coming to be with us here on earth. It is a very mystical moment when an entire church overcrowded with people praying aloud suddenly becomes silent. The awareness that Our Lady is with the visionaries at that very moment, no matter where they are, spoke to my heart in a special way.

SIDENOTE: In Chapter One I wrote that my parents "insisted" we prayed the rosary as a family. I've come to realize how grateful I am for their strength in that battle—and believe me, sometimes it was a battle! When my Mom said it was time for the rosary, suddenly everyone had homework that just "had to get done!" However, the rosary always won out, and I am so grateful that my parents understood the importance of teaching their children to pray.

In Medjugorje I finally understood that the rosary is not what I thought it to be as a child—a long, drawn-out repetition of prayer. It is not just a mantra of meaningless Hail Marys. It is a beautiful meditation on the life of Christ and His sacrifice for us . . . His sacrifice for me. It is a time of remembering the Joyful Mysteries, beginning with the Incarnation, when the Word of God became flesh; the Sorrowful Mysteries of Jesus' passion and death on the cross; the Glorious Mysteries of His resurrection and ascension into heaven; and the Mysteries of Light (added by Pope John Paul II in 2002), including Jesus' first public miracle, when, at His mother's request, He changed water into wine, His proclamation that the Kingdom of God is at hand, and His transfiguration.

The rosary tells the story of salvation that is to be passed on from generation to generation. The recitation of the Hail Marys while meditating is very soothing and allows me to think of each step that Christ took for me. At the same time, we are asking Our Blessed Mother, who was with Jesus all of this time, even at the foot of the cross, to intercede for us with her Son, as she did at the wedding at Cana.

When I arrived in Medjugorje, a day's journey from home, and found the whole world praying the rosary the same way I had been taught to pray it as a child in my parents' home, it was a special moment of understanding that we are truly united in prayer. I realized that I was among the many children of the world whose parents had taught them this beautiful way to pray.

The evening Mass was somewhat difficult to grasp the first time I went. It seemed particularly long, not only because it was but also because it was difficult to follow. All of the prayers as well as the homily were said in Croatian. Helen's family had put together a booklet with the prayers and songs in both Croatian and English, which made it somewhat easier to follow. Nevertheless, it was a long evening of prayer. What struck me most at this Mass was the fact that about eighty priests from all over the world concelebrated. Twelve to fifteen of the priests took turns reading the Gospel, each in a different language, so that everyone present would hear God's word spoken. When the Gospel was finally read in English, I understood!

Seeing that many priests huddled so close together on the altar was a beautiful sight. We were told this wasn't even the busy time of the year. The spring, summer, and early fall bring many more pilgrims to Medjugorje because of the warmer weather, and with them come many more priests. For this reason, a beautiful circular outdoor altar with a tented canopy has been built. It stands directly behind St. James Church. This altar is large enough to accommodate many more priests. The number of pilgrims who worship together in those months can reach into the tens of thousands, particularly on the feast of the Assumption, August 15, and on the anniversary of the apparitions, which is June 25. The Youth Festival, which began in 1989 and is held each year from August 1 to 6, has brought together as many as fifty thousand worshipers in recent years. Along with the pilgrims, there are more than five hundred priests concelebrating each night!

As of June 2012, the Catholic Church has not yet made its final decision on the authenticity of these apparitions. However, in the early days, Pope John Paul II encouraged priests to go to Medjugorje because people were going there, confessing their sins, and returning to the sacraments. The fruits of Medjugorje are abundant. It has been called "the World's Confessional," and Mom and I have witnessed this.

When the Mass was over, the Glorious Mysteries of the rosary were prayed, and then the priests blessed all religious articles that had been brought to Medjugorje or purchased by the pilgrims in the village. The evening concluded with prayers for healing of the sick. That evening's schedule, we would learn, has occurred every day of the week since the early days of the apparitions. It was a very long evening for our first experience!

SIDENOTE: Mom and I have now been to Medjugorje together six times. Improvements have been made over the years to make everyone feel welcome in this little village, especially at the International Mass each evening. Nowadays, if you bring a small AM/FM radio with earphones, or purchase one when you

get there for a very reasonable price, you can hear the evening
Mass translated into your own language. At the Information
Center near the church you can get a printed list of all the
languages and the radio station that coincides with each one.

Our first full day had been incredibly long. The evening had turned
to rain and after the International Mass Mary Pinto was feeling both
tired and overwhelmed. The long journey had taken its toll, her
camera had been stolen, and she went to bed feeling certain she
shouldn't have come.

Chapter Five

FRIDAY, November 16, 1990

The Sun Will Come Out Tomorrow . . . and it did!

We woke up Friday morning to sunshine. After the morning Mass, a woman approached Mary Pinto. She told her she was so sorry because the day before she had accidentally picked up Mary's camera, thinking it was her own. She said she recognized Mary when she saw her again because she remembered her bald-headed child. We came to learn that Helen's unashamed confidence in Our Lady was something we should learn to imitate. Helen doesn't speak as though Our Lady "might" hear our prayers. Helen speaks because she knows Our Lady is listening.

Helen's Mother . . . and Helen's Daughter, Miriam

Although we had signed up for this trip in order to travel with Helen Sarcevic, it turned out that her mother had become ill. When we were settled in Medjugorje, Helen had to go to her mother's home in Zagoria, near Zagreb, to be with her. For the next few days, Helen's daughter, Miriam, was the guide for our trip. Miriam is most likely a few years younger than me, which was thirty-one at the time. I was impressed by her because she never seemed unnerved or impatient with our large group. She was a beautiful guide with a gentle personality. Whenever you spoke to Miriam, even if there were others in line to speak to her, she always gave you her undivided attention. The apple doesn't fall far from the tree in that family!

Throughout the week I was Miriam's helper. I was happy to assist whenever she needed me, whether to pass out information to the group or to run a quick errand of some sort. We quickly became friends on that trip and Miriam confided in me that she had a prayer request. She had a boyfriend named Rick. She loved him very much and she knew he

23

loved her. Rick, however, was also wondering if God was calling him to the priesthood. I thought that Miriam's prayer request would be for Rick to choose her. She surprised me when she said her prayer request was for Rick to know what his calling in life would be and for her to be able to accept God's will. I learned a lot from Miriam that week. The long story made short: Miriam and Rick have now been married for many years and have two beautiful children.

Fr. Petar Ljubicic . . . a very special priest

On Friday afternoon we went to one of the other buildings located on the grounds of the church. Fr. Petar Ljubicic was to be the speaker.

Before I continue I need to explain the messages of Medjugorje. As I mentioned earlier, Our Lady has been coming to the Medjugorje visionaries daily since June of 1981. On March 1, 1984, Our Lady began giving weekly messages on Thursdays through the visionaries to the people of St. James Parish. Then, on January 25, 1987, Our Lady began giving a message on the 25th of the each month instead, through Marija. These messages were intended not just for the parish of St. James but for the world—for you and me. To the present day, this message can be read by all because it is translated into many languages and sent out over the Internet on the day it is given.

From the beginning, Our Lady also began revealing ten "secret" messages to each of the six visionaries. When Our Lady has revealed all ten secrets to a visionary, she no longer comes to them daily. The first of the six visionaries to receive all ten secrets was Mirjana. On December 25, 1982, Our Lady revealed the last of the secrets to her. She then told Mirjana that she would no longer come to her on a daily basis but would instead come to her once a year, on March 18. The second visionary to receive all of the secrets was Ivanka, on May 7, 1985. Our Lady now comes to her once a year, on June 25. Jakov received the tenth and final secret on September 12, 1998. Our Lady now appears to Jakov once a year, on December 25. To make it even more confusing to remember, in addition to all of the above, on August 2, 1987, Our Lady appeared unexpectedly to Mirjana. At that time she told Mirjana that she would come to her on the second of every month for the rest of her life. As of this writing, the remaining three of the six visionaries—Ivan, Marija, and Vicka—still see Our Lady daily, and each has received nine of the ten secret messages.

The secrets are about events that are to take place in the future. The visionaries have said they do not like the word *secrets* because it sounds too spectacular. However, it is the English word closest to their Croatian words that mean "future events of which we cannot yet speak." The visionaries have not discussed the secrets except to say two things. The third secret has to do with a permanent, indestructible sign that will be left at the sight of the first apparition. When this event takes place, many will believe, but it will also be too late for others. The other secret we have been told a little about is the seventh. Our Lady has said that because of prayer and fasting, the seventh secret, a chastisement, has been alleviated.

Fr. Petar Ljubicic was sent to Medjugorje by the communist government of Yugoslavia to straighten out the people there. They felt he could put a stop to all that was happening. As it turned out, Our Lady told Mirjana to choose one priest to whom the secrets would eventually be revealed, when the time comes. Mirjana chose Fr. Petar Ljubicic. He is a holy priest, and as he spoke to us we could see he was very sincere and concerned about the condition of the world. Again we heard the messages of prayer, conversion (of heart), fasting, and so on, and about how important it is to implement them in our lives.

A Special Apparition on Friday Night . . .
announced by Slavica

On Thursday we were told there would be a special apparition the following night on Mt. Krizevac at 10:00. We later understood that Our Lady often invites the visionary Ivan and his prayer group to climb Cross Mountain to pray for peace. The pilgrims are always invited to join them and often several of the visionaries are present.

Our group was very excited to climb the mountain. From down in the village and anywhere in the surrounding hamlets, you can see what looks like a small cross at the peak of this mountain. In reality, this concrete cross stands thirty-six feet tall. The cross was built in 1933, in celebration of the nineteen hundredth anniversary of Christ's death and resurrection. On the crossbar is written "33–1933." Learning that this cross was built during a period of communist rule, we came to appreciate the strong faith of the Croatian people. There was no worn path to the top of the mountain at that time. The fact that the distance from the bottom to the top is a mile and a half meant that men and women had to climb the mountain innumerable times carrying buckets of sand, water, and tools to make this a reality. We were told that when Pope Pius XI heard that the Croatian people were building this cross, he sent a relic (or sliver) of the true cross of Jesus, which resides in the church of the Holy Cross of Jerusalem in Rome.

Climbing Mt. Krizevac . . . no one goes it alone

As excited as the rest of the group was to climb, Mary Pinto was exhausted and said there was no way she was going to be able to carry Stephen all that way. We had heard that the path to the top was difficult, with loose rocks and large boulders all along the way. It was a cold November evening and the trip was already wearing on Mary. I remember telling her that she wouldn't have to carry Stephen at all. I knew that, with our large group, we could all take turns. With Mary convinced that her new family would be there for her and her son, we all set off on Friday at 7:30 P.M. to climb Mt. Krizevac.

As we had been warned, it really was a challenging climb. We were bundled up in coats, hats, gloves, and scarves. Because it was November, it was dark when we began the climb, so we headed out with flashlights in hand. Someone handed Mom a large stick found along the path to guide her steps—after all, she was sixty-seven years old!

I took several turns carrying Stephen. He was not a slight five-year-old. He was very solid and carrying him was quite a challenge. I had to make sure my footing was secure with each step. However, there was something in this exercise that was uplifting. Carrying Stephen felt more like a gift than a burden. Just knowing that we were all helping Mary and being so close to this sick little boy opened my heart in a new way. It was as if I wanted to suffer for him—as if my suffering somehow would bring him joy. Admittedly, I was getting quite tired when along came our guardian angel, Brother Terry, who had been climbing solo as he approached our group. Brother Terry, a complete stranger, became a newfound friend to Mary. Seemingly over six feet tall, with his grey hooded robe covering his large frame, he took Stephen out of my arms and, like someone who was carrying a large bag of clothing, moved swiftly up the mountain as if he did this every day!

We arrived at the top along with hundreds of others. With this many people huddled together in the darkness, we were thankful that we had begun the climb early.

Miracle Pictures . . . lots of them!

As we stood around chatting, a man I didn't know came over and began showing me "miracle pictures." He said they were taken by pilgrims in Medjugorje who, when they got their pictures developed, found images in them that weren't there when the pictures were taken. One picture that really touched my heart was of the open tabernacle in St. James Church. It had been taken during the consecration and in the tabernacle was what appeared to be the face of Christ. I don't know if this was a miracle picture, but it caught my attention.

The Rosary, the Wind . . . and the birds

It was around 10:00 when the prayers of the rosary began. Someone on the top of the mountain was leading them and the rest of us were responding. It was a beautiful night and being on top of that mountain without the distraction of street lights or the light from the villagers' homes, the stars were more brilliant than I had ever seen them before. It seemed like we could see millions of them and they appeared to be closer than ever.

As I said, it had been a workout climbing the mountain. Any time you set out in the cold all bundled up, if you are moving around the way we did, you build up a lot of body heat. We had removed our hats and unzipped our coats. That's why the next memory stands out as something of importance.

As the rosary was being prayed by the hundreds or more who were in attendance, suddenly, without warning, the prayers came to a stop. At the time I didn't understand why it had gotten so quiet. What I do remember is that a cool breeze was suddenly upon us. I remember thinking how wonderful it felt because we had been so warm and here was this refreshing breeze. I stood there and savored that moment.

Another detail that stands out in my memory is that during the time of silence the birds suddenly came alive and burst into song. I remember making a mental note of the odd hour for birds to be singing. Was it the sudden silence that awakened them, or was it something else?

The prayers resumed and when the rosary ended, there was acknowledgment among those present that Our Lady must have come. Pilgrims began making their way down the mountain. Mom and I had to wait for the crowd below to thin out before we could begin our own descent. Finally we turned on our flashlights and, step by step, began our slow, steady climb downward. We had no worries; after all, there were hundreds, maybe thousands, of people on the mountain.

Excuse Me . . . can you help us down this mountain?

We didn't realize how slowly we were moving. Maybe it was because one flashlight had died and we were taking our steps more cautiously now, but suddenly Mom and I realized there was no one else around us. I am sure the others did not realize as they headed down the mountain that we had fallen behind. For some reason, neither of us seemed concerned. Although we realized we could possibly go the wrong way and end up on a wrong path in the dark, we weren't really worried.

As we walked along, Mom noticed that a short distance ahead there seemed to be two dark figures waiting along the side of the path. That was the one time we felt some anxiety. We had heard about gypsies who sometimes rob people when they are alone, and we certainly were alone. Well, there was nowhere to go but down, so we trusted God and moved forward. With one flashlight between us, we slowly approached the two dark figures, who were sitting on a large rock.

"Excuse me," one of them said in English, "our flashlights have gone out and we are afraid to move on without one. Do you think you could help us down the path?" We felt immediate relief as we realized these were not gypsies at all; in fact, they were two women just like us. They shared that they had said a prayer to God, asking Him to send a Guardian Angel to help them down the path. They told us He did better—He sent two! It was nice to know that God was using us to answer a prayer.

The slow descent became even slower as the four of us made our way down the rocky hillside with one flashlight. You would think that these circumstances would put a damper on our evening, but they had just the opposite effect. We laughed and talked all the way down the mountain.

At 1:30 in the morning we saw the first signs of light ahead and knew that we had arrived back at the base of the mountain. At first I thought it kind of strange that our "family" hadn't come looking for us, but sometimes you just have to have faith—or a beer! That's exactly what they were doing. We came upon them sitting at a little café at the base of Mt. Krizevac enjoying beer, wine, and coffee and going over the night's events. When we came out of the darkness and into the light (literally), they all broke into applause. We were exhausted and it felt so good to join the group for refreshments before heading "home" to Ivanka's house.

Lou from Atlantic City . . . and the wind

I don't remember Lou's last name. He worked as a bouncer at a casino in Atlantic City. He was one of the pilgrims from our group staying at Ivanka's house. As we sat at the base of Mt. Krizevac, he shared that he hadn't had a strong faith before coming on this trip. He'd come to Medjugorje out of curiosity. He'd heard about it from a friend and had decided to take the trip on his own. He told us he had never had much time for prayer or church, but there he was in Medjugorje, and his "mountaintop" experience had been a memorable one.

He told us that as he arrived at the top of the mountain, he didn't realize it at first but he was standing right near the visionaries. When they began to pray the rosary he was right beside them! With the stars shining so brightly at the top of the mountain, he could see their faces clearly. At one point the wind began to blow around them, and then it was as if the wind "stopped on a dime." At that very moment, the visionaries went down on their knees right in front of him! He could see them clearly during their time with our Blessed Mother. He could see their faces and their lips moving, but he could no longer hear their voices. As never before, he felt as if spontaneous prayers were being pulled out of him. He said he couldn't have stopped them even if he had wanted to.

It was obvious that he was overwhelmed by the whole experience. He said he was not going to be the same person when he returned to the casinos of Atlantic City.

We returned by cab to Ivanka's house. Our group was very charged up and although it had been a beautiful night, a sudden sadness came over me as we arrived back home. Maybe it was exhaustion setting in, maybe something else. I felt like the gifts that others were receiving— such as the sun spinning or being near the visionaries during the apparition on the mountain—were huge. They all seemed so excited, yet I was feeling a sudden heaviness in my heart. I was missing my family and wondering why I was there. I shared my feelings with Susan Minnick, one of the women from our house. She suggested that I pray to Our Lady and ask for tomorrow to be a better day. She said I just needed a good night's sleep, and she promised she would pray for me too. After praying, I fell asleep quickly.

Chapter Six

SATURDAY, November 17, 1990

Marija's House . . . she blessed me too?

On Saturday morning, after a good night's sleep and a delicious breakfast, we were told that the visionary Marija would be speaking to the pilgrims from the front steps of her home. When we arrived, the crowd was already gathering, but somehow we ended up standing right in front of her as she spoke.

Marija was a gentle and soft-spoken young woman. There were three interpreters at her side. Each time she said a sentence or two, her words were translated into English, then into German, and then into a third language, and so the process began. We soon forgot about the translators, however, because her message was so beautiful. She began, "Last night Our Lady blessed everyone who was on the mountain. She also blessed those at the base of the mountain who could not make it to the top." She went on to say, "Our Lady says to pray for peace in your own heart first. She says you should then pray for peace in your family, your community, and then the world. In order to have peace in our families, we must first have peace within our own hearts. It must begin with each one of us."

Something stirred in my heart that morning as Marija told us that Our Lady had blessed everyone who was on the mountain. Suddenly I remembered how I had felt the wind cooling me, and how, just as suddenly, the prayers had stopped and it was assumed Our Lady must be there. I remembered how the birds were singing at that late hour and I felt that even they must have known of her presence. We had been on the mountain when Our Lady appeared and she had blessed us. Susan Minnick was right! It was going to be a wonderful day.

Apparition Hill . . . the tree and the rosary

After listening to Marija, we walked through the fields to where Our Lady had appeared to the children in the early days. The official name of the hill is Podbrdo, but it is more commonly known as Apparition Hill.

It was a beautiful day as we made our way up the rocky path. The climb was not as difficult as it had been in the dark the night before on Cross Mountain, with its huge boulders. Apparition Hill is not as steep, yet it has many small, loose rocks, so we had to be equally careful with our footing. As we climbed we prayed the rosary. An Italian artist had donated beautiful bronze depictions of the mysteries of the rosary, which stand approximately four feet wide and four feet high. These had been placed along the hillside all the way to the top. We stopped at each mystery, prayed an Our Father and the other prayers, and then moved along to the next one.

Throughout the village there are many families who own sheep and goats. We often saw the goats roaming about freely as we climbed. They were walking along the path or lying on the sun-warmed rocks. At first these visitors intimidated us, but we soon learned they were not interested in us at all.

Halfway up the hill we paused to offer some prayers for friends and loved ones. As each person offered their prayers of petition for family members experiencing divorce or for a loved one who was ill, I was suddenly aware of my self-centeredness from the beginning of the trip. There was Mary, with her five-year-old son who could die from cancer, hoping for a cure, and here I was, looking at my rosary day after day to see if the chain had turned gold. I felt so ashamed. I had been looking at this rosary as somewhat of a lucky charm rather than as a tool for prayer. I decided I needed to let go of whatever had been blocking me from God's grace on this trip. To do that, however, I had to let go of the one thing I owned that I believed had belonged to my Grandmother. I knew what I had to do, so without prolonged hesitation I hung the rosary on the branch of a nearby tree and walked away. It was time to let God lead the way.

Without warning, tears began to flow. I know it's been said that I cry easily; however, this was different. Something new began to stir in my heart at that very moment, and I know the reason was twofold. I felt I had left something precious behind, so those were sentimental tears, yet there were more tears flowing than necessary for that one act. The rest were tears of cleansing, a washing away of my self-centeredness, allowing me to be open to God's grace and become someone new. I cried as I climbed Apparition Hill, but it was a kind of crying that I had never experienced before. There was true sorrow in these tears and they needed to flow in order to wash away my old self and give me a new beginning.

When the tears subsided, I felt a great sense of peace and excitement. Each mystery of the rosary was more meaningful than ever before. Each prayer offered by others was joined by my own silent prayers for them. I prayed for my own family and friends and for many people at home who had asked for prayer. When we arrived at the top of the hill, I sat quietly alone, feeling as though I could stay there forever. The sun was warm; life was beautiful. I could see the entire valley below and there, in the distance, was St. James Church. It was as though I was seeing the world around me for the first time.

Dr. Mark . . . like a brother

After a period of rest at the top of the hill, it was time to return to the village. Heading down the path, I had been walking with Dr. Mark, another of the pilgrims staying in Ivanka's home.[2] In my 1990 journal I wrote the following:

"I walked with Dr. Mark from our group. I said to him, 'Going home is going to be so hard because around here, you can turn in any direction and talk to any person about God, Jesus, or Mary. You can't do that at home.' Mark said his little girl is very supportive of him and I asked if he had her picture. He showed me a picture of his eight-year-old daughter and there was a little boy with her who looked to be about six months old. I said, 'Is this your son?' He answered 'Yes, that's part of my problem.' He then told me his son was abducted eighteen months ago. Unexpectedly, the tears began,

---

[2] Some names have been changed for the sake of privacy.

as though one of my own brothers had just delivered this news. He went on to say that he and his wife were divorced and then he had a relationship with a woman. They moved in together and had a child—the little boy. Their relationship fell apart and they were having a custody battle when she took off in July of 1989. He hasn't seen her or his son since. He's here asking the Blessed Mother for forgiveness and help in finding his son."

I remember this conversation and the feeling of sadness that came upon me as soon as Mark said his son had been abducted. Suddenly his pain became my own and I experienced a friend's sadness as never before. The tears were so sudden and unexpected that I knew I was experiencing the kind of selfless love we are to have for others. I had to apologize for their sudden onset because I knew they were not what he needed at that time.

Miracle of the Sun . . . was it?

That same afternoon, Mom, Carol Catalano, a woman from Scranton, Joe McCormick, and I were walking from Ivanka's home through the fields to St. James Church for the evening Mass when we experienced what some might say was the miracle of the sun. Joe pointed out that the sun was spinning and, of course, we all looked. We were able to look directly at the sun and could see what looked like a Host, or the wafer of bread used in the Mass, right in the center, shaking as if to block out the blinding sun. Behind the Host, the outer edges of the sun were golden and shining. Seeing this, I realized that something inside me had changed. Now, instead of "looking" for a miracle, I doubted that I was worthy to experience one. I doubted myself until later that night when Mary, Stephen's mother, said, "Did you see how beautiful the sun was today? I couldn't even look at it as it was going down! It was so bright!" I knew I had been able to look directly at the sun at that same moment.

Eucharistic Adoration . . . a beautiful experience

Twice a week, another form of Catholic worship takes place at St. James Church in Medjugorje: Eucharistic Adoration. The Catholic Church believes and teaches that during the Mass, the bread and wine become the body and blood of Jesus Christ. He gave Himself to us at the Last Supper (read Matthew 26:26–28) and it is for this reason that we worship His true presence in the Eucharist (read John 6:25–59). Although the duration of the evening Mass and other prayers is approximately three hours every night, twice weekly, after a break of an hour or so, worship resumes from 10:00 to 11:00 P.M. in the form of Eucharistic Adoration. For those who have been to Medjugorje and experienced this beautiful time of worship in the warmer months, when it takes place at the outside altar, the Adoration I describe here will be somewhat different because it took place inside the church.

As was recommended, Mom and I arrived at the church a half an hour early so that we would be able to sit in a pew. However, the pews were already full and the only open floor space remaining was in the center aisle, three-quarters of the way toward the back. We quickly took our places there and the area behind us filled in until the church was packed to overflowing.

As the time approached for Adoration to begin, we noticed a group of at least twenty men filtering into the area around and close to the altar. We later learned that these men were from the Community Cenacolo, a drug and alcohol rehabilitation center located right there in Medjugorje. The men who live there have committed to remain in this community for three years in order to become free from their addictions. As it says on the medjugorje.usa.org website, *"Many are drug addicted desperate lost souls. Passing through the doors of Community Cenacolo, these young people begin to feel hope and a sense of being, and family. The aim of the community is to renew the family: to help the families meet Jesus Christ, Savior and Redeemer, also to bring support, love, healing and faith."*

Once the men were in their places around the altar, the most beautiful music began to play. The violin left the greatest impression on me, but it was the combination of many instruments that was so beautiful, and it continued until the Most Blessed Sacrament was placed in the gold Monstrance, a vessel in which the consecrated Host is exposed for adoration and then placed upon the altar. Fr. Slavko Barbaric, a priest who spoke eight languages, then led us in prayer. Once again, as with the reading of the Gospel at Mass, words were spoken into the microphone in one unfamiliar language after another. When he spoke in English, his simple words stirred my soul and his prayers became my own—words such as these: *"Jesus, I want to thank you for dying on the cross for me"* and *"I am sorry for the times I have been less than loving. I want to love others as you desire me to love."* For several minutes, Fr. Slavko prayed this way, until translations in eight languages were accomplished.

After the prayers, there were several minutes of complete silence, which is hard to imagine in a church filled with more than a thousand people. It was adoration in a way I had not experienced it before. Repetition of music, prayers, and silence were the order of worship, which continued for one hour, while everyone in the church was kneeling. The floor of the church is marble. Mom, as always, was a beautiful example for me as she knelt in adoration for a solid hour on that hard floor. It would be hard to forget this profound experience of worship.

St. James Church with Mt. Krizevac in the background

A more recent photo of St. James Church

Mom and me before our climb up Mt. Krizevac

Mary Pinto, Stephen Felgendreger, and Brother Terry Messer

Bronze sculpture of the fourth Joyful Mystery on Apparition Hill

Bronze sculpture on Mt. Krizevac of the fifth
Station of the Cross: Simon helps Jesus carry His cross

The front of the cross on Mt. Krizevac reads, "To Jesus Christ, the Redeemer of the human race, as a sign of our faith, love and hope, in memory of the 1900th anniversary of the Passion of Jesus."

The back of the cross on Mt. Krizevac reads,
"33–1933"

This cross marks the place where Our Lady appeared to Marija and gave her this message: "Peace, peace, and only peace must reign between God and man and among humankind."

Mom captured the moment that I (center of picture) was contemplating leaving Nan's rosary on the tree

Mom having quiet prayer time on Apparition Hill

Mom on Apparition Hill

Mom climbing Mt. Krizevac

Me on Mt. Krizevac

Confessions being heard along the side of St. James Church

Fr. Sempko with pilgrims

Pilgrims gathering for the evening rosary and Mass

Veneration of the Cross

Many priests concelebrating at the English Mass

Fr. Slavko Barbaric during Adoration

A quiet afternoon outside St. James Church

The statue of Our Lady that stands in front of St. James Church

Mom and Visionary Ivanka

Visionary Marija and her translators

Visionary Vicka speaking to pilgrims

Miriam translating for Fr. Petar Ljubicic

Miriam speaking with Visionary Ivan's mother

A typical scene in Medjugorje in 1990

One of the grape vineyards found throughout the village

Not-yet-ripe kiwifruit

Stephen and the five Marys

The moment the Holy Spirit came upon me in the
church in Switzerland, captured by Mom

Nan's rosary

The statue belonging to my mother
that we used for the family rosary

Chapter Seven

SUNDAY, November 18, 1990

Mt. Krizevac . . . born again

Early Sunday morning, our group prepared to climb Mt. Krizevac again. This time we would walk in the daylight, so it would be an easier journey. As on Apparition Hill, fifteen bronze sculptures that replicated the Stations of the Cross, donated by an Italian artist, had been placed along the path for pilgrims to stop at and prayerfully meditate on the passion of Our Lord.

It was on this climb to the top that, for the first time, I felt in my heart the combined suffering of Jesus and Mary. I realized how much Jesus had suffered for my sins and I saw how Mary, as His mother, also suffered because of my sins. She was with him every step of the way. At each station, we read from a beautiful booklet on the Stations of the Cross, and each time my heart ached because of the pain and suffering caused by my sins. Jesus and Mary had suffered so much because of me.

I had heard that no Medjugorje pilgrimage is complete without confession. I was hesitant to go to confession because it had been many years since the last time I'd gone. I tend to think it had been at least fifteen years, but it could have been more. I decided to ask Fr. Sempko, as we climbed the mountain, if he would hear my confession sometime that day. He told me to look for him at the top of the mountain. If he was in a quiet place and not with another pilgrim, he would hear my confession then. I wasn't expecting that quick of a reply, but it was going to happen whether I was ready or not! Ask and you shall receive!

When we reached the top, I was in awe of the magnificent view. As far as my eyes could see, in every direction there were mountains. It felt like I was on top of the world. After spending some time alone, I finally got the nerve to look for Fr. Sempko. I found him resting on a large rock and he welcomed me with a warm smile. I told him I didn't know where to begin because it had been a very long time since my last confession. He suggested we take a look at the Ten Commandments, and comfortably moved me into a confession that was more like a conversation with a friend. I can't remember exactly when the tears began to flow, but they did. I talked and cried and let go of things I had forgotten were part of my past. It was the first time in my life that I remember feeling truly sorry for my sins. The slow climb up Mt. Krizevac and the meditations on the Stations of the Cross that were so powerful resulted in my acknowledgment that my sins had been the cause of so much pain for Jesus and Mary and I was truly sorry. I had never really understood that my behavior, my actions, and my words toward others, or lack thereof, had such an impact on my relationship with Jesus. When Fr. Sempko ended my confession with "Your sins are forgiven; not only the sins you have just confessed but even those you have forgotten to confess. All of your sins before this moment are now forgiven," I felt cleansed as never before. It was a new beginning. At that moment, I felt as though my life was starting over.

As Mom and I headed down the mountain, I shared with her that I had just had the most powerful confession of my life. I told her I felt "as clean as snow" and "like a newborn baby." I had no idea at the time that I was quoting Psalm 51:7.

Truly, that was the moment I was *"born again . . . in Medjugorje!"*

Now, whenever I read the following scripture passage, these words have new meaning:

John 3:1–8

There was a Pharisee of the Jews. He came to Jesus at night and said to him, "Rabbi, we know that you are a teacher who has come from God, for no one can do these signs that you are doing unless God is with him." Jesus answered and said to him, "Amen, amen, I say to you, unless one is born from above, he cannot see the Kingdom of God." Nicodemus said to him, "How can a man once grown old be born again? Surely he cannot reenter his mother's womb and be born again, can he?" Jesus answered, "Amen, amen, I say to you, unless one is born of water and Spirit he cannot enter the Kingdom of God. What is born of flesh is flesh and what is born of spirit is spirit. Do not be amazed that I told you, 'You must be born from above.' The wind blows where it wills, and you can hear the sound it makes, but you do not know where it comes from or where it goes; so it is with everyone who is born of the Spirit."

Fr. Jozo's Church . . . in Siroki Brijeg

We arrived back in the village around noon. Because it was Sunday, the English Mass was at 12:15 P.M. After yet another beautiful Mass filled with the Holy Spirit, we returned to Ivanka's home for our 2:00 dinner. Following dinner, we had some free time and Mom and I were considering heading back to the shops near the church to look for souvenirs to bring home. Suddenly, a cab pulled up out front and someone asked if we were interested in going to see Fr. Jozo (meaning Joseph) at his parish. It was a last-minute decision, but Mom, Maryann Gillespie, and I got into the cab and were off on our next adventure. Even if Fr. Jozo didn't have an English interpreter, we could at least see his church and the beautiful statue of Our Lady that everyone had been talking about.

SIDENOTE: Fr. Jozo was the pastor of St. James Church in Medjugorje when the apparitions began in June of 1981. He had been in Germany and returned on the third day of the apparitions to find his parish in turmoil. Hearing that six children had spoken of having visions of the Blessed Virgin Mary, he was not immediately convinced. After all, why would the Mother of God come to his parish?

There came a day, it is told, when Fr. Jozo was inside the church alone. He was praying to God, asking Him to let him know how to handle this situation, and wondering if these apparitions could be authentic. As he prayed, he heard a voice speak to him: "Go out and protect the children." He immediately got up and went outside to find the children running in his direction. They were frightened and begged him to help them hide because the communist police had been chasing them. All morning they had been running from them and hiding in the fields.

Fr. Jozo immediately told the children to go inside the church. Anticipating that the police would soon be coming his way, he sat down on the steps and waited. The police soon arrived and asked him one question: "Have you seen the children?" He said yes and was ready to say more when they ran off in the direction they assumed the children had gone. From that moment on, Fr. Jozo believed the children.

Soon Fr. Jozo's church was overflowing on a daily basis. The communist police began placing plainclothes officers in the church during the Mass in order to accuse the priests of stirring up the people with their homilies. They brought these accusations against Fr. Jozo, accused him of aiding the children, and sentenced him to prison for three years. After eighteen months of beatings and torture, they freed him, on the basis that he would no longer be the pastor of St. James Church in Medjugorje. This is why he had a parish in Siroki Brijeg at the time of our pilgrimage in 1990.

A forty-minute ride along the backroads finally brought us to a beautiful church in Siroki Brijeg. As our cab pulled up, we noticed that there were only a few cars and two busses in the parking lot. As we were getting out of the cab, our friend Janet, from Vermont, came out of the church saying, "Hurry up! Fr. Jozo is blessing everyone!" Janet had arrived earlier with three others from our group. Once we were inside the church, we learned that the busses belonged to a large group of Italian pilgrims and Mass was to be celebrated in their language. The seven of us weren't sure if we should stay, but we would definitely receive a blessing from Fr. Jozo.

Slain in the Spirit, Blessings and Deliverance . . . we weren't going anywhere!

As we walked up the aisle, a very strange sight lay ahead of us, literally! There on the floor at the front of the church were several people lying on their backs. As we got closer, I noticed that people were walking past them as if unaware of their presence. What was going on here? I saw that as Fr. Jozo blessed people, a man stood directly behind the person being blessed. Several times as Fr. Jozo was blessing pilgrims, they fell backward into the waiting arms of the man standing there. He carefully lowered them to the floor and moved behind the next person being blessed.

Being quite unfamiliar with what was happening, I was uneasy with the whole situation. Suddenly, as Fr. Jozo began to bless a woman wearing a purple coat, she began to struggle. My first thought was that she was having a seizure of some kind, because she shook her head and body very hard; but it also seemed as though she didn't want to be blessed. She quickly moved on and went back to her seat. A woman in a red coat had a similar reaction and then moved on to be seated.

Not fully understanding what was going on in this church, we went up for our blessing without incident and then back to our seats. The Italian pilgrims were seated in the first several rows of the church. We left some empty pews behind them when we took our seats.

The commotion began when the woman in the red coat started to have what seemed to be a coughing fit. She coughed so violently that we thought she would be sick. Then the woman in the purple coat also began to cough. The two women continued coughing for some time. A man had his arm tightly around the shoulder of the woman in the purple coat, but she kept bending down in her pew and coughing. All of a sudden she began to scream things, and the woman in red was doing something too, but from where we were sitting, behind her, it was hard to tell what it was. I'm not sure what triggered it but suddenly three or four men pinned down the woman in purple right there in the pew. Their bodies were shaking as they struggled to hold her down. Fr. Jozo approached very calmly and guided the woman in red to a room behind the altar.

We watched with horror as the men trying to hold down the violent woman in purple seemed to be shaking from head to toe. A man standing in front of the group of Italians had obviously just asked everyone to pray for these women. The entire group immediately began to do so.

Fr. Jozo came back from the room behind the altar and approached the woman in purple. As he came near her, she swung at him and missed as he quickly backed away. At that moment, I started to believe what I really didn't want to believe was happening. As Fr. Jozo had come for the second woman, I had heard a horrible deep-throated laughter come from her as she continued to resist everyone around her. After she swung again at Fr. Jozo, he approached her a third time. For some reason she went with him this time, practically falling onto him and using him for support. He walked her into the same room behind the altar.

The Mass was then celebrated by an Italian priest and continued through to the end without interruption. Although we did not speak the language being spoken in that Mass, the atmosphere was clearly one of concern, fear, and anticipation. The prayers were being lifted up with such emotion that even though there was a language barrier, there was no denying their power. After Holy Communion we seated ourselves in the first pew directly behind the group of Italians on the left side of the church. When the Mass ended, as is the custom of the Croatian people, we prayed seven Our Fathers, seven Hail Marys, and seven Glory Be's.

When these prayers were finished, the woman wearing the red coat came out of the room behind the altar and went back to her pew. We were now seated across from her rather than behind. We could see her smiling as she spoke to the people in her group, and I assumed, on the basis of everyone's faces, that she was well and that her friend in the purple coat was also going to be fine. She then returned to the room behind the altar. Five minutes later, she again came out of the room and stood with her back against the wall to the left of the altar. She had a look of happiness and peace on her face. She then turned toward the crucifix and bowed in what looked to be a gesture of thanksgiving.

Then the woman in the purple coat, who I had assumed was mentally ill when I first noticed her resisting the blessing, came out from the room behind the altar. She was smiling and looking very peaceful and calm. A priest—not Fr. Jozo—motioned to the woman in the red coat to approach the microphone. As you can imagine, the stillness in the church was incredible and everyone's attention was on this woman. Smiling thankfully, amid deep breaths she said something in Italian. Not knowing the language but looking at the smiling faces of all the people in the church, I could only guess. I said to the woman next to me, in the hope that she understood English, "I do not understand." In her Italian accent she said to me, "She was delivered."

Then the woman in the purple coat came to the microphone and said something in a very gentle voice. I turned to the woman beside me once more and asked, "Can you tell me *exactly* what she said?" She answered, "She wants to forgive all of the people she's not been able to forgive and she desires forgiveness from those she's hurt." There were cheers and applause from everyone in the church. I can say one thing for sure: I was very thankful I had confessed my sins that morning!

"So if you are offering your gift at the altar, and there remember that your brother has something against you, leave your gift there before the altar and go; first be reconciled to your brother, and then come and offer your gift." (Matthew 5:23–24)

"Then Peter came up and said to him, 'Lord, how often shall my brother sin against me, and I forgive him? As many as seven times?' Jesus said to him, 'I do not say to you seven times, but seventy-seven times.'" (Matthew 18:21–22)

In the cab on the way back to Ivanka's home, Maryann explained the following: It seemed to her that these women had allowed Satan into their lives by the choices they had made. When Fr. Jozo attempted to give them a blessing, the evil inside these women resisted the presence of the Holy Spirit. Sometimes when a person is blessed and receives the Holy Spirit willingly, he enters into them so powerfully that they actually pass out. This is called "resting in the spirit" or "being slain in the spirit." It is said to be a very peaceful time in which the person feels God's grace and presence. Now we understood why there were people lying on the floor of the church. We understood that this was a *good* thing.

This is not what took place for the women who did not receive the Holy Spirit; they went back to their pew with the evil stirred up inside of them. Satan was still with them, which was clearly displayed in the awful laughter, strange voices, and striking out at the priest that we had witnessed.

I recorded the details of this event in my journal that night. That journal entry finished this way:

"This is not something we imagined. There were seven of us from our group who witnessed this together and now we all know the grip that Satan can have on a person's life if they are unable to forgive, to ask forgiveness, to love God or to pray. Mary, our Mother, says prayer is the greatest weapon against the devil. Our lives have been changed by this event."

As you can imagine, we talked the entire ride home. I don't know what time it was when we arrived back at Ivanka's house but we were quite motivated by the experience to stay together late into the night. Earlier in the week Ivanka had told us that we were welcome to help ourselves to her homemade wine. We decided it was a good night for a bottle of red wine. A group of us stayed up for quite some time and shared the day's experiences. We were in no rush to turn out the lights that night. As I wrote in my journal, "Mary, our Mother, has said that prayer is our greatest weapon against the devil," and pray we did!

Dr. Mark . . . is there a doctor in the house?

The next day was a special day for Dr. Mark. It was Monday afternoon and Fr. Jozo had been invited to come and speak at St. James Church with his interpreter. He had just begun his talk when someone handed him a note. After reading it he announced, "If there is a doctor present, please come to the side door of the church." Mark, who had been sitting nearby, immediately got up and disappeared out the side door. This announcement raised concern in everyone in the church because at that time there was no hospital in Medjugorje and the closest doctor was in Mostar, at least a thirty-minute drive away.

Hearing the people murmuring, Fr. Jozo came back to the microphone and said with a smile, "If a person is going to die, what better place than in Medjugorje?" As odd as it may sound, everyone erupted into applause, and then Fr. Jozo suggested we say a prayer for whoever needed it at that moment. I was beginning to realize, in this little piece of heaven, that there's more to life than living here on earth.

That afternoon, as our group gathered around the large dining room table for dinner, Mark finally returned.

Mark's Story . . . doctor or priest?

Mark shared with us that as soon as he left the church he was put into a car that immediately took off at high speed. It carried him along the winding roads to a nearby village. He had no idea where he was going and wondered momentarily if he had risked his life getting into that car.

The car quickly arrived at a small Croatian home where he was brought inside. What Mark found there was an adult male lying in a bed, curled up in the fetal position. He seemed to be having chest pains and shortness of breath. The man did not speak English, nor did Mark speak Croatian; however, the driver of the car served as an interpreter for both of them.

Mark began asking the man questions, trying to determine the reason for his symptoms. Soon after, there came a knock on the door and in walked Fr. Jozo. He had come to see if he could help. Mark felt somewhat relieved, and later could not adequately describe his joy at being in the presence of this holy priest. He had hoped to meet Fr. Jozo and speak with him but assumed he'd never get the opportunity. With only two days left in our pilgrimage he had resigned himself to the fact that the only time he would spend with Fr. Jozo would be in the church, listening to him talk along with hundreds of others—and then he had been called away! Suddenly and without prior notice, he was in a complete stranger's home and practically alone with Fr. Jozo. The driver served as interpreter while Mark had a wonderful conversation with Fr. Jozo.

The short story about the person lying in the bed was that originally he was complaining of chest pain and shortness of breath and it was thought he was having a heart attack. As it turned out, he was having a major anxiety attack, which resulted in similar symptoms. Apparently his life had become overwhelming for him and he was having great difficulty handling it. As the father and husband of his large household, he had kept all of his worries to himself. In the end, he did not need a doctor at all but someone to talk to, someone to show him they cared. Mark stayed for several hours and talked with the man and Fr. Jozo. By the time he left, the man was smiling and thanking God for Mark's visit.

Mark shared with us that the entire day had been a gift for him. Many years ago, before medical school, he had entertained thoughts of becoming a priest. He had considered it for a time but it had never happened. This day had allowed him to experience not only the role of doctor but also the role of someone who was able to be there for another person in a way that priests often are. The man in the bed, who was in pain when Mark arrived, only needed someone to listen to him, and on this particular day the person who had been sent to his side was Mark. The man had not needed a doctor at all but instead someone to show he cared and to help him know God was there for him. For a day Mark felt like Fr. Mark rather than Dr. Mark.

Chapter Eight

MONDAY, November 19, 1990

Monday, November 19, 1990 . . . our last full day

Before we knew it, our last full day had arrived. How could this be? So much had happened in such a short time. My life had taken an amazing turn in just one week. When I left home, my greatest hope was to see the visionaries or hopefully be near them when they had an apparition. Maybe I would get to see the sun spin or my rosaries would turn to gold. As it turned out, God gave us a double blessing! Not only did we get to see a visionary, we had stayed in her home! The rest, I suppose, was just God's way of getting my attention—so that I would come to understand what His true gifts really are.

The sun spinning and rosaries turning to gold had become less important as the week progressed. The picture that the man had showed me at the top of the mountain on Friday night, of the face of Christ in the tabernacle, had made a great impression on me. I have to admit that for several days, each time we were in church for the morning and evening Masses, I intentionally looked in the tabernacle during the consecration, and each time it was the same result: an empty box with a pure white interior.

Vicka's House and Ivan's Mother

How does one explain the visionary Vicka? She does not have the worldly beauty that would attract you to her if she passed you on the street; she's actually rather plain looking. However, there's a joy that comes from Vicka's face, from her smiling brown eyes, that just makes you smile back. Her beauty comes from within, a beauty that words can't describe. Maybe the following explanation will help. One time, the visionaries asked Our Lady, "Why are you so beautiful?" She answered, "I am beautiful because I love. If you want to be beautiful, you must love." It is the pure love that Vicka exudes that makes her so beautiful.

As Vicka spoke, I knew her words were meant for all of us, but it was as if she was speaking directly to me. Her words penetrated my heart. As Vicka spoke, she made eye contact with everyone present, and when she looked at me, I could tell she really wanted me to "hear" Our Lady's messages. She stressed the importance of faith, conversion, fasting, and especially peace. She then prayed over some people, as she always does. She prayed over Mary and Stephen for a very long time. Being in her presence was a special gift.

After being at Vicka's home, on our way to the 10:00 morning Mass we passed by Ivan's mother's house. Ivan was in the United States at the time. His mother was out front and Miriam introduced us to her. Someone in the group asked, "How did you feel the first time your son came home and told you what he saw?" Miriam translated her response: "I like to keep my thoughts private. Many people take an answer and in their own words the answer gets changed all around." She was very kind but we understood her need for privacy.

Miracles Do Happen . . . when you least expect it

It was to be the last English-speaking Mass of our pilgrimage. The week had been amazing, with priests from all over the world giving beautiful homilies. We heard from priests with accents from Ireland, England, and Nigeria. The Holy Spirit had been filling us up every day. As I shared earlier, because of the picture the man had shown me on the mountain Friday night, throughout the week I had been looking into the tabernacle hoping to see something special, but always to no avail. On this, our last day, I had finally let go of that thought. After hearing Our Lady's messages of love from the priests and visionaries, after being born again on the mountain and receiving the grace to start my life over, I was no longer looking for that miracle.

The Mass continued and it was time for the consecration. Without intentionally looking that way, my eyes were drawn to the open tabernacle. I hadn't thought of it ahead of time, it just happened. My heart all but stopped when I no longer saw an empty white box. The inside of the tabernacle now appeared to be a soft grey color and in it I saw the profiles of the faces of Jesus and Mary. My first thought was that maybe all the excitement of the week had gone to my head, so I looked away. When I looked back, I expected the tabernacle to look normal, but the image was still there. A second time I looked away and then back again, only to find that the vision remained. My heart was pounding. I tapped the shoulder of Maryann Gillespie, who was kneeling right in front of me. She turned around and I said, "Look in the sanctuary!"

You have to understand: I had really been a "baby Christian" before this trip. I had always been Catholic, but I hadn't known a-n-y-t-h-i-n-g!!! I was calling the *tabernacle* the *sanctuary!* She said, "Where?" I pointed and said, "In the sanctuary!" She looked quite confused and said, "Do you mean the tabernacle?" "Yes, there!" She turned to look and I watched as she covered her mouth with her hand. She looked back at me with disbelief and tears in her eyes. I decided at that moment that as soon as Mass ended I would ask her to tell me first what she saw, before I told her anything. Then I would know for sure if I had really seen something or if I was just imagining things.

After the consecration and during the Our Father, I had another memorable experience. As always, I reached out to those on either side of me to hold hands during this prayer. The man standing to my right was a tall string bean of a guy with a long ponytail down his back. As we held hands and prayed, I felt so connected to him, as if I knew he was my brother in Christ. Because I knew Jesus was present there at that moment, I could feel His love in this complete stranger. I now understood what Jesus meant when He said: "For where two or three are gathered in my name, there am I among them" (Matthew 18:20).

My heart continued to pound and, as I received Jesus in the Eucharist, I felt closer to God than ever before. I was sure He was right there and that it was Him I was receiving.

As soon as Mass had finished, I asked Maryann to tell me what she had seen. I was surprised when she said she had seen "the face of Christ and then the face of a child. It became the face of Christ again, and then the face of a child." I didn't understand. I had seen something completely different. I told her I had seen the profiles of both Jesus and Mary in the tabernacle. I asked, "Why would we each see something completely different?" She said, "I don't know why you saw what you did but I am a pediatric nurse. At the moment I saw Jesus' face become the face of a child, I felt in my heart He was telling me that He is there in every sick child I take care of. That's Him!" Her explanation made it clear to me that what God gave each of us that day was meant for us individually. It also helped me to set aside a thought I'd had during my vision, and that was, "Is someone producing this image somehow with a video projector just to make people believe in this?" I didn't think I was worthy of a miracle such as this and that is what went through my head for a moment. I am also inclined to believe that the evil one was trying to discourage me from accepting this gift. God made certain through Maryann's words that I believed and understood.

As a child I was taught that Jesus is present in the Eucharist, and although I didn't understand, I believed. Seeing His image alone would have been enough for me to accept this truth, and now I understood His presence more fully. I knew He was there. However, since that day so long ago, I have come to believe that the reason I was given the vision of both Jesus and Mary in the tabernacle was so that I would never doubt Mary's presence in Medjugorje. She is there because Jesus has asked her to come. Her greatest desire and reason for coming is to lead all of us to her Son, who was crucified for our sins. She was with Him at the foot of the cross; why should I not believe she was with Him in this church? The visionaries have said that Our Lady says, "Whenever the faithful adore my Son, I am present."

Chapter Nine

TUESDAY, November 20, 1990

You've Experienced Heaven on Earth . . .
now take it wherever you go

It was still dark at 5:15 Tuesday morning. Ivanka had given us an early breakfast and packed each of us a bag lunch of thick slices of homemade bread, delicious cheese, an apple, and cookies. She gave us each a wonderful hug; I told her I would miss her, and I meant it. As our tour bus pulled away from her dimly lit home, she stood waving from her driveway until we could see her no more. The tears began to flow. My sadness at the thought of leaving this piece of heaven was overwhelming. How could I have come to love a place so much in such a short time? How could I want to stay here any longer when I hadn't seen or spoken to my husband or children in an entire week?

I had tried to call home one day midweek. The only opportunity to do so (in 1990) was when the one public phone booth, located on a street corner in the center of the village, was in operation, for a few hours in the middle of each day. As a result, the line of people waiting to use this phone was always long. The one time I was able to call, to my great disappointment our answering machine picked up and the only voice I got to hear was my own! I left a message, which I found out later they never heard, so they didn't even know I had called.

The Rainbow . . . I set my bow in the sky as a sign

We were on our way home and it was the first leg of our long journey. We were flying from Zagreb to Zurich. I have found that with all good gifts that come from God, Satan will also come and try to destroy your peace. I had started talking to Mom about the fact that we needed to go home and share this week with our whole family. We needed to tell them *everything*. As we sat there, I began having such thoughts as

"What if we don't make it home?" and "What if our plane crashes?" I'd just had a life-changing experience and I needed to go home and share it with my family, but what if we didn't get there? At that moment, I happened to look out the window and could see the shadow of our plane against the clouds. A beautiful rainbow was encircling the shadow. I wondered (again) if I was just "seeing things." Just then someone from our group who was sitting in the seat behind me said, "Look at that rainbow around our airplane's shadow!" It may seem silly to some but this was my confirmation that Our Lady was taking us safely home. The Bible says in Genesis 9:12–13 that God said, "This is the sign of the covenant that I make between me and you and every living creature that is with you for all future generations: I have set my bow in the clouds, and it shall be a sign of the covenant between me and the earth." I had no worries the rest of the way.

Come, Holy Spirit . . . fill our hearts

It was Wednesday, November 21, 1990. Fr. Sempko was at it again, but this time he didn't ask me to sing. He asked me to be a reader during our last Mass of the trip, which took place in Switzerland, and for some reason, without hesitation, I answered yes. Whenever I had to stand in front of people and speak, I felt very uncomfortable. As usual, my heart began to pound at the idea. I told Fr. Sempko I was getting nervous and he said, "Just ask God to help you read the words the way He wants them to be heard." I did exactly that and then I asked Our Lady to help and stop my nervousness.

My heart was pounding as I stood and walked to the front of the church. I felt as though everyone could see it beating. As soon as I was in front of the microphone, the Holy Spirit took over. I didn't understand it at first but something that felt like a gentle current entered my body at the top of my head. It began at the follicles of my hair and slowly passed down through my entire body, all the way to my feet. At that very moment, my pounding heart settled and I read effortlessly. I felt as though I was reading to my children at bedtime. This was incredibly unusual because anytime before this, if I was nervous and my heart was racing, it would take a good fifteen minutes after I had finished for my heart to settle. This time, my heart was calm while I was reading. I sat down knowing that the Holy Spirit had come upon me. This is a gift I will remember always.

Mom told me I had read very well and Fr. Sempko later said, "If I meet up with you a year from now and you tell me you're not a reader at your church, I am going to be very disappointed!" Fr. Sempko would be happy to hear that I did become a reader shortly after I returned home to New Jersey, and I loved it!

Chapter Ten

WEDNESDAY, November 21, 1990

⁙

The Last Leg of the Trip . . . Nan's rosary

The last leg of the trip home was the longest—a six-hour flight. As Mom and I sat there, I must have been talking about having left what I believed was Nan's rosary hanging on a tree because, unexpectedly and quietly, Mom began telling me a story about the day Nan died that brought tears to her eyes.

Mom was visiting Nan at my Uncle Jim's house, where she was staying. Nan hadn't been well for some time and was sitting in a wheelchair in the bedroom. When it was time for lunch, Mom gently removed Nan's rosary from her hands and placed it on a nearby table before taking Nan out to the dining room. After lunch, Mom and her sister Connie went for a walk. On their way back, an ambulance had passed them and stopped in front of Uncle Jim's house. As it turned out, Uncle Jim had become concerned about Nan while they were gone and had called for the ambulance, which then took Nan to the hospital. Nan's health quickly failed and she was unresponsive to most of her visitors. Within a few days, she died.

I can still see the sadness on my mother's face as she shared how bad she felt that she had taken Nan's *black* rosary out of her hands that day and that Nan had died without it. I don't remember ever seeing such sadness in my mother's eyes as when she told that story. However, it was at that moment that I realized that the *blue* rosary I had left on the tree in Medjugorje could not have belonged to Nan. What I actually gave to God on that hillside was my heart.

On Christmas that year, Mom handed me a small box. Inside was a delicate and much worn black rosary. The wood of the cross, which no longer held the image of Jesus, was cracked from years of handling and the imprint on the gold medal at the center point of the rosary was worn thin from years of Nan's thumb caressing it. Mom's gift to me that Christmas was more precious than anyone will ever know.

The Last Entry in My Journal . . . go and live the messages

The last entry in my 1990 journal reads as follows:

> "We're on our way to Kennedy airport in New York and should
> arrive in about five and a half hours. It will be a very sad good-
> bye as we leave the many wonderful people who were our
> family for the week. I pray that each of us can go home and live
> the messages we heard all week. I also pray that Jesus and Mary
> will stay by my side and help me to be strong when I feel weak,
> because the people at home are not like the people in
> Medjugorje—not yet."

I'd had no warning about the atmosphere we would return to at Kennedy
Airport. It certainly did not resemble the peace we'd encountered when
we arrived there a week earlier—or was that a lifetime ago?—and saw
Helen's welcoming smile waiting inside the front door.

In just one week's time I had experienced God's love more
completely, it seemed, than I had in the first thirty-one years of my
life. I had emerged from the womb of Medjugorje and was now about
to take my first breath. However, I have learned that when you give
your heart to God, you can expect a visit from His adversary—and he
didn't wait long to drop by!

We arrived at Kennedy the day before Thanksgiving; one of the
busiest travel days of the year! Here I was, floating along on my
oblivious little cloud, when the storm hit! There was pushing and
shoving as travelers with uptight faces rushed by trying to get to their
next plane or destination without delay. All sorts of unnecessary
hand signals flew from one stranger to another as we made our way
to the luggage area. It had been our intention to say our good-byes
there after retrieving our suitcases; but it didn't turn out that way.
Mom and I soon realized that some of our new friends had connecting
flights, so they had moved on to other areas of the airport before
we'd had a chance to say good-bye. The rest of us had to find the
drivers who were waiting to take us to our homes. So we rushed
through our hugs and tears as we parted from friends who would be
forever remembered.

As Mom and I waited by the curb with our luggage, exhausted from the long journey, the smiling faces we had seen all week seemed to be fading from our minds. We stood alone in a sea of people, with horns honking all around us. We had left our little piece of heaven and arrived in . . . another place.

I Want to Go Home . . . now!

I remember vividly that once we were on our way home, I really *needed* to be home! The van from the airport would be dropping us off at Joey's parents' house on Fulmer Street, where our journey had begun. It seemed impossible that it had been just over a week since we had departed. That day seemed so long ago. Was our long-awaited pilgrimage really over? The closer we got to his parents' house, the more I missed Joey and the children and the more anxious I was to see everyone. I couldn't understand how I had been gone an entire week without talking to any of them. The need to see them was suddenly overwhelming.

As we came upon the turn onto Fulmer Street from the boulevard, I was so happy. Unexpectedly, however, the driver didn't slow down and went right past the turn! I was patient for a short time, thinking he was going to come in another way, but when he continued to get farther away, I told him he had missed the street. He said he planned to take us home last and we'd be there after he dropped off the other passengers. Typically this wouldn't be a problem, to anyone, but I needed to see my family . . . now. As we got farther away, I asked the driver if I could use his phone to call Joey at the house to tell him of our delay. He did let me use his phone, and then for some reason, after his next stop; he took us right to the house. It was the longest few blocks I have ever traveled.

We finally arrived at my in-law's home. As we pulled up, Joey and the kids, my Dad, and Joey's parents all came out to greet us. It was the most joyful reunion of hugs, kisses, and tears, and the beginning of a very long night of sharing.

Chapter Eleven

SOMETIME AFTER MY RETURN

⁎⁎

Mt. Holly, New Jersey . . . God's gifts continue

You might think this story ended upon our return, but it had only just begun. It was necessary to move back into the realm of this world, but things would never be the same. Returning to my life as a wife and mother was not difficult. I had a wonderful husband and three beautiful children to return to, and a newfound love for God that would see me through all things. A few things about me had changed and one in particular was a new desire to attend daily Mass. I have always loved to sleep in a little, but now I wanted to start each day at Mass and receive Jesus as often as possible. Joey was very understanding and adapted to this change quite well, although I'm sure it wasn't easy for him. I began to attend the daily 7:00 A.M Mass at Sacred Heart Church in Mt. Holly, New Jersey. Our children were young; Matthew, the oldest, attended afternoon kindergarten. So, with the children still asleep, Joey was able to get ready for work uninterrupted, and I was able to go to Mass without interfering too much with the day's routine.

One cold Friday morning in winter, after having attended Mass each day that week, I awoke early. My first thought was to stay home that day. Curling up under the covers for another hour sounded like a nice idea, yet I also wanted to go to church. I almost stayed home that day, but I got myself up and off I went.

After the Mass, I began my drive home. As I was sitting at a traffic light, suddenly my attention was drawn to the side-view mirror. The sun was brilliantly orange that morning, but what had caught my eye was that it seemed to be shaking. I wondered if my idling car was causing my mirror to vibrate. I checked the other side-view mirror, only to see the same thing happening. I then looked in my rear-view mirror, and could clearly see that the sun was shaking. As it had in Medjugorje, my heart began to race in wonder at what was happening. Once again I had doubts, because I felt unworthy to receive a special gift from God.

After all, why now? Why here? I turned fully around in my seat to look out the back window, and was able to see, without mirrors, that the sun was indeed pulsating and now beginning to spin.

I became aware that the light had turned green, so I continued on, but as soon as I came to a side street that I was able to turn onto, I pulled over so I could look again. Maybe, I thought, it was all in my imagination and I wouldn't see it again.

I parked my car, and what I saw then I will try to describe. If you are familiar with the sparklers on sticks that are often used on the Fourth of July, then you can visualize twirling one of those sparklers in a circular motion with your wrist and leaving a trail of sparks following the main light. As I watched the sun, which was an extremely bright orange ball of fire, it began to spin like a pinwheel, with a trail of orange lights following it. My heart pounded wildly and, as you've probably guessed, I began to cry. What was going on here? Why did I just see this? Why did God give me this gift on a Friday morning in Mt. Holly, New Jersey? I was not imagining this; I know what I saw, but how was I going to explain it?

When I got home, I was visibly shaken and shared the whole experience with Joey. Understandably, he was somewhat skeptical. He asked, "Why do you think you saw that?" I told him I honestly didn't know.

It was at that moment, however, that I realized I didn't have to be in Medjugorje to experience God's gifts. He can make His presence known to me—to all of us—at any moment of any day.

My only answer to why God would have blessed me in such a beautiful way that morning was that maybe He was saying thank you— *"Thank you for putting me first in your life!"*

EPILOGUE

Why I Wrote This Book . . . two reasons

Although I wrote most of this book from memory, when I checked my 1990 journal for accuracy, I was amazed at my recollection of these events. I now know that even if I had not written them down, these memories would have been forever ingrained in my heart. My reason for putting them into a book was twofold.

First, from the time of our return, I have known that my pilgrimage to Medjugorje was a gift from God. I have also felt that He gave it to me expecting me to share it with others, as I have desired to do. He had lit a fire in my heart and I could not keep it to myself (Matthew 5:14–16). My children have grown up hearing about Medjugorje. These stories are not new to them; in fact, they may be all too familiar. To paraphrase John 4:44, you can't be a prophet in your own home. I have wanted my children to know my story—all of it. I have written it down for Matthew, Emily, Patrick, Christian, John, Mary, and Theresa, in the hope that someday they'll hear it again . . . for the first time.

My second reason for writing was, of course, my Mom. However, I want to first say thank you to Albert Hendel. Dad, if you hadn't given Mom your complete blessing on these trips, it's possible I may never have gone to Medjugorje. I hope, however, that you did experience a bit of heaven right here in Lancaster when Ivanka brought Our Lady's messages to us in December of 2008.

Mom, we have traveled together to Medjugorje six times (in 1990, 1996, 2000, 2004, 2006, and 2009). Although this book gives *my* point of view and shares *my* memories of our first pilgrimage together, I wanted to give you the opportunity to remember and experience again the joy we experienced in sharing a little piece of heaven on earth. I love you, Mom. It has meant the world to me to walk with you through the streets and vineyards of this village, to climb Apparition Hill and Cross Mountain so many times while holding your hand in mine. In all those years you never once complained that it was too much or too difficult; you climbed up and down those hills with a perpetual smile on your face—no matter what the weather! How about the lightning storm and drenching rain on Apparition Hill in 2009? I asked, "Are you nervous?" With rain running down your face and with that simple grin we all love, you answered, "About what?"

Having you by my side at Holy Mass over the years, while receiving Jesus both inside St. James Church and at the magnificent altar outside, has been the greatest gift of all. How many times did we get to hear a sermon given in a foreign accent by a priest so filled with the Holy Spirit? How often did we experience the music of the choirs from Ireland singing "Lady of Knock"? Adoration of the Blessed Sacrament under the stars with five thousand people, along with the beautiful music of the violinist, stirred our hearts like never before. I saw your unending joy at being in the place where Our Lady has been coming for so many years. What an odd sight it was the first time I saw you sitting on a rock at the top of Apparition Hill, resting. I don't have many childhood memories of you, the mother of ten children, just sitting and relaxing. Yet there you were, seated so serenely, taking in peace-filled breaths as you looked out at the village below and at Cross Mountain in the distance. You have worked so hard your whole life and you are a wonderful mom. To see you sitting there as if you could stay all day was a gift in itself. Together we have laughed and cried along the way, and I will always thank God that we have had this time together.

After Medjugorje . . . a few notes

Mary Pinto and Stephen Felgendreger. On April 27, 1991, several months after our pilgrimage, Stephen Felgendreger was taken home to heaven. His mother, Mary, did not receive the miracle she had asked for, yet she says many miracles did happen. It was through Stephen—a young child with such simple faith—that many, many people came to experience God's love. Mary's church, St. Anthony's, began a weekly prayer meeting specifically intended for friends to pray for Stephen. People who had been far from God came to this church to pray with them. When Stephen died, many of these people said if it hadn't been for this little boy, they might have stayed away even longer.

I kept in touch with Mary through letters and phone calls for several years after that pilgrimage. As it turned out, Mary and Brother Terry developed a lasting friendship. He did work at a homeless shelter for men in New York. On occasion, Mary would go and visit Brother Terry. One such trip to New York was very helpful to her in her acceptance of God's will for her son.

Mary had been told that Mother Teresa of Calcutta was going to be in New York that weekend. She stood in a long line of people waiting to say hello or just to shake the hand of this saintly woman. She was holding a small picture of Stephen, which she showed to Mother Teresa. When Mother Teresa saw the picture, she thought Mary was showing her a picture of her sick child. Mary tried to explain that in fact her child had died, but she didn't think Mother Teresa understood. As she began to walk away, she felt a tug on her sweater. She turned around and saw it was Mother Teresa who had stopped her. Mary realized that Mother Teresa had indeed understood when she asked, "Have you given him to Jesus?" Mary replied, "He has him. I didn't have a choice." Mother Teresa then took Mary's face in her hands and said, "You must give this child back to Jesus so that he can be an 'angel' in heaven for peace." Mary said it was those words that helped her accept God's will for Stephen.

Several years later, Joey and I received an invitation to Mary's wedding. She had been dating someone who she said was a good and Godly man. As Joey and I were on our way to the wedding, he asked me what the groom's name was. I said, "Joe Mallon." He said, "That's funny. I knew a guy in high school named Joe Mallon, but he went into the seminary." Lo and behold! He had come out of the seminary and there he was standing at the altar marrying my friend Mary. Mary and Joe went on to have a daughter and two sons.

Dr. Mark. Years after I met Dr. Mark, I saw him at a retreat. He told me that when he returned from Medjugorje he was invited to speak about the trip at an event. After speaking, he was then invited to give more talks. At one particular event, a man approached him. He said he was the father of the woman who had given birth to Mark's son. When he'd heard that Mark was speaking he had decided to come and listen. He wanted to let Mark know that he knew where his daughter and Mark's son were living. They were both doing well; she was a good mother and she was taking good care of Mark's son. The man said he would have to get in touch with his daughter before he could let Mark know where they were. That was the last time I spoke to Mark about it, but it gave me hope that he was on his way to finding his son.

Brother Terry. Brother Terry Messer became a priest in 1994 and is now Fr. Terry. He is one of the founding members of the Franciscan Friars of the Renewal.

Acknowledgments . . . from my heart

First of all, I thank God for never giving up on me. Thank you, Heavenly Father, for your patience and unconditional love. Thank you for your healing sacrament of reconciliation, which led to my conversion on Mt. Krizevac, and for sending the Blessed Virgin Mary to lead us to Jesus.

I also thank Mary, the Mother of Jesus, the Queen of Peace. Thank you for leading me to your Son, and for loving all of us so much that you would be willing to come to this ungrateful world for so many years. Please don't give up on us. There are so many whose lives have been changed and so many more to come to your Son.

Thank you, Jesus. Thank you for being patient with me through my teenage years, and beyond, and for waiting for me. I know now that you were with me every step of the way. Thank you for all the joy you have given me in my life since I came to know you. Thank you most of all for being willing to suffer and die on the cross for my sins.

Thank you, Joey, my dear husband and friend, for being willing to "let go and let God." As our family has grown and changed, you have always supported me when I have felt called to return to Medjugorje. With three children left in your care during my first trip, five on my second, and seven by the time I made my third pilgrimage, it's a good thing the pattern broke at that point—otherwise we'd have fifteen children by now! You have unselfishly allowed me to experience God's grace at my "home away from home" time and again. I can't imagine that many men would have honored that sort of request from their wife and I hope you know how truly grateful I am. I know God has blessed us greatly because of your willingness to say yes. Our trip together to Medjugorje for our twenty-fifth wedding anniversary, in 2007, was a prayer answered. My desire to go there *with you* and experience this amazing place and its people together was so strong and I thank God for that pilgrimage. To climb the hills and experience the Mass at St. James Church with you was a longing I've had since my first trip there in 1990. Everything in God's time!

I have been a stay-at-home mom for more than twenty-five years and, with that, your stay-at-home wife—a title I love. Writing this book has taken me away from you and the children for more hours than we ever expected and I am grateful for your patience. We know it was never my intention for this memoir, which I wrote for our children, to "go public," but sometimes God takes us on the most unexpected journeys. Thank you for letting go, once again, and allowing me to walk with God. I hope you know how much it means to me each time you tell me you are "so proud of me." Becoming a mom was something I had always desired; becoming an author was never even a passing thought. Both have been deeply rewarding.

Matthew, Emily, Patrick, Christian, Johnny, Mary and Theresa—my children—thank you all for encouraging me along the way to continue writing. Your words of support have meant the world to me. Thank you for putting up with "just one more story" when I have excitedly shared a memory that has just come back to me. Thank you for being there for me; you are each a blessing. It was a great joy to travel to Medjugorje with Patrick in 2004, when he was fifteen years old; and this year, God willing, Mary Elizabeth and I will be there for the Youth Festival. I pray that one day each of you will experience this piece of heaven right here on earth—the place where I was . . . *born again.*

Thank you, Alice Rowan, my editor, publisher, and newfound friend in Christ. It was purely "God-incidental" that your name was given to me twice within one hour of hearing "you need to publish this book!" You are gentle, kind, smart, compassionate, and such a gift to me. I am so glad we met, not just because you are the wonderful editor that you are, but because it has made the journey to becoming an author that much more enjoyable. We have shared many laughs, hugs, and even a few tears along the way and it's all been a gift to me.

Thank you to all of my family and friends, too numerous to mention, who took the time to read my original manuscript and encouraged me to publish it. Siblings and in-laws, friends both young and old, and those with whom I've traveled to Medjugorje—you all gave the same advice: publish it!

Last but certainly not least, I thank Maureen and Fred Lomady for sharing their experience of conversion through Medjugorje. It was you who first spoke the name of that little village to me, and you who first shared with me Our Lady's messages of peace, prayer, fasting, conversion, and reconciliation. Thank you both from the bottom of my heart. It changed my life and saved my soul. You are truly my brother and sister in Christ.

ZBOGOM! Walk with God!

What's Next . . . Psalm 121

What comes next? I can't be sure where God is taking me on this book-writing adventure. However, I can tell you this: each pilgrimage I have taken was unique, and all of them have been a gift from God. If I do write another book, I already have the title in my mind. It will be *Psalm 121 . . . I Lift Up My Eyes.* Here's why.

Since I returned from my first pilgrimage to Medjugorje, I have never forgotten how it changed my life. Six years and two children later, I was being called once again to visit my home away from home. The problem was, there had been a war in that area of the world and for several years very few pilgrims had traveled there. Finally, in 1996, peace had come to the area and, with Joey's blessing, I was ready to return. The night before our departure, we had a prayer meeting in our home, with friends praying the rosary for Mom and me to have a safe and faith-filled journey.

After our friends left that night, Joey came to me with tears in his eyes and said, "I just want you to come home safely to me." The war had ended but there was still some unrest in certain parts of that country. I had not been aware of his concern. After Joey left the room, I looked at the Bible on my kitchen counter. It was open to the Psalms. Not knowing the Bible very well, I said, "Lord, please give me a passage to leave with Joey that will make him know I'm safe." I thought to myself, which Psalm? Immediately pulling an idea out of nowhere, I said to myself, "My birthday is January 21. OK: Psalm 121!" So, what does it say? I was once more in awe of God's perfect answer to prayer. Psalm 121 says,

I lift up my eyes to the hills, from where will my help come?
My help comes from the Lord, Who made heaven and earth.
He will not let your foot be moved; He who keeps you will not
    slumber.
He who keeps Israel will neither slumber nor sleep.
The Lord is your keeper; The Lord is your shade at your right
    hand.
The sun shall not strike you by day, Nor the moon by night.
The Lord will keep you from all evil; He will keep your life.
The Lord will keep your going out and your coming in
From this time on and forevermore.

I took the Bible to Joey, told him what had just happened, and read the Psalm to him. Before I left on my trip, I wrote Psalm 121 down for him to look at whenever he was worrying about me.

On the airplane the next day, I was a little anxious about having left him in such a state of worry. Several weeks before my pilgrimage, Joey had put together a tape of songs for me to listen to on the long journey. I put my headphones on and turned on the music. My heart began to race as I heard a beautiful voice begin to sing, "I lift up my eyes to the hills, from where does my help come?" This was music Joey had chosen for me several weeks before. I turned the cassette case over and looked at the titles of the songs, which Joey had listed. There on the back of the case was "Psalm 121, by Susan Ashton." God had answered yet another prayer! It gave me chills to begin this trip with such confirmation that God was again going to be there every step of the way.

My next book, then, should I find time in my life as a busy wife and mother to write it, will be called *Psalm 121 . . . I Lift Up My Eyes.*

Appendix A

About the Visionaries

IVANKA IVANKOVIC-ELEZ was the first to see Our Lady on June 24, 1981. She was born on June 21, 1966, in Bijakovici. Ivanka's prayer mission from Our Lady is to pray for families. Her mother, Jagoda, died in April 1981. When the apparitions began, Ivanka asked the Blessed Mother about her mother. Our Lady said that her mother was with her in heaven. God has allowed Ivanka to see and speak to her mother several times over the years. Ivanka had daily apparitions from June 24, 1981, until May 7, 1985. On that day, Our Lady confided to her the last of her ten secrets. Our Lady told Ivanka that for the rest of her life she will have an apparition every year on June 25, the anniversary of the first apparition. Ivanka is married and has three children.

MIRJANA DRAGICEVIC-SOLDO was born on March 18, 1965, in Sarajevo. Her prayer mission from Our Lady is to pray for all unbelievers. She had daily apparitions from June 24, 1981, until December 25, 1982, when she received the tenth and final secret from Our Lady, making her the first seer to receive all ten secrets. After that, Our Lady appeared to her once a year on her birthday, until August 2, 1987, when Our Lady also started appearing to Mirjana on the second day of each month to pray with her for all unbelievers. Mirjana is married and has two children.

VICKA IVANKOVIC-MIJATOVIC is the oldest of the visionaries. She was born on September 3, 1964, in Bijakovici and comes from a family of eight children. Her prayer mission given by Our Lady is to pray for the sick. For her, the daily apparitions have not yet stopped. Our Lady has confided nine secrets to her so far. Vicka is married and has two children.

IVAN DRAGICEVIC was born on May 25, 1965, in Bijakovici. He has two younger brothers. His prayer mission given by Our Lady is to pray for priests and the youth of the world. Our Lady has appeared to him every day since June 24, 1981. To date she has confided nine secrets to him. He resides half the year in Medjugorje and half in Boston, Massachusetts. He is married and has four children.

MARIJA PAVLOVIC-LUNETTI was born on April 1, 1965, in Bijakovici. Her prayer mission given by Our Lady is to pray for the souls in purgatory. She has three brothers and three sisters. Our Lady appeared to her for the first time on June 25, 1981. She still has apparitions every day and is the visionary to whom Our Lady gives the public message to the world on the twenty-fifth of each month. Our Lady has confided nine secrets to her so far. Marija is married and has four children.

JAKOV COLO is the youngest of the seers. He was born on March 6, 1971, in Bijakovici, and was only ten years old when the apparitions began. His prayer mission given by Our Lady is to pray for the sick. He had daily apparitions from June 25, 1981, until September 12, 1998, when Our Lady confided to him the tenth secret. Our Lady literally raised Jakov because his mother died when he was very young. She now appears to Jakov only once a year, on Christmas Day. It was very difficult for him to accept that he would no longer see Our Lady every day. He wondered how he would continue. He struggled for months until, through prayer, he realized that he was now like everyone else who does not see Our Lady. She is with each one of us always, he says, and we can experience her in our hearts. Jakov lives in Medjugorje, is married, and has three children.

Ivanka Speaks in Lancaster, Pennsylvania

As I mentioned in Chapter Three, eighteen years after my first pilgrimage I had the privilege of hosting Ivanka in my home. On December 5, 2008, she spoke at St. John Neumann Church in Lancaster, Pennsylvania. The evening gathering began with the rosary, followed by Holy Mass, and then Ivanka's personal testimony about Our Lady's messages and the early days of the apparitions. The following transcript was translated by Darlene (Sarcevic) Milas.[3]

I greet you with all of my heart because I am so happy to be with you here tonight and to have celebrated Holy Mass together with you, and in the same way I am so happy that you wish to hear Our Lady's messages. Because for twenty-seven years now heaven has been opening up and has been calling us, and it has been giving each of us love in a special way, because each one of us is special to God in his or her own way. And for twenty-seven years now I have been asking myself, "God, why have you chosen me?" and I still don't know. I do not have an answer to that question. But I have accepted this great, immense gift which is at the same time a great immense responsibility. And I continuously pray to Dear God to give me the strength to follow the path that he has intended for me. Because twenty-seven years ago I was only a child. I was fifteen years old.

On the twenty-fourth of June, 1981, it was the feast day of St. John the Baptist, and so we spent that day just like any other feast day. In my village, it was tradition on the feast day, no one did work. Everyone went to Mass as a family, and after Mass the parents would rest, the adults, and the children would be able to play. And so a few of us girls made plans to meet together on the outskirts of the village. And so my friend Mirjana and I were the first to arrive. At that time, Mirjana was living in the city of Sarajevo

---

[3] Transcribed by Mary H. McCafferty on December 10, 2008

and I was living in the city of Mostar. So having met back in our parents' village for the feast day, we were talking about what had happened to us during our school year. We became tired of waiting for the other girls to come, and so we started to make our way back to our homes.

As we were walking back, something was drawing me to look towards the hillside, and when I looked up in the hill, I saw the Mother of God. And so I touched my friend and I said, "Mirjana, look up there! It's Our Lady!" But she did not even look and she said, "How could you say such a thing! What do you mean? Our Lady?" And so then I stayed silent and we continued on towards our homes.

And so, on our way, we met with a girl, Milka, who had gone to look for some lost sheep. As soon as she saw my face she asked me, "Ivanka, what happened to you? Why do you look this way?" And walking back towards that spot I told her what I had seen. When we came back to that spot, those two girls also saw what I had seen. About four hundred meters up the hillside from us, Our Lady was standing and she was motioning to us with her hands. But our emotions were so much in turmoil within ourselves that we were afraid to go closer to her.

At that time, another girl, Vicka, had come closer to us and she could see that something unusual was happening with us. We said to Vicka, "Come over here quickly! We have seen the Mother of God!" When she heard what we said, she took off her shoes and ran straight home. On her way home she saw two boys, both of them named Ivan,[4] and told them what was happening. They came back towards us and they too saw what we were seeing. Even though there were now more of us there, we still were afraid to go closer. I don't know exactly how long we were standing there.

Little by little we went to our homes. A couple of us went to the very first home we came to. And so we entered that home, and in

---

[4] Milka and one of the Ivans saw Our Lady only on the first day, June 24, 1981. The next day, Jakov and Marija saw Our Lady for the first time; these two, along with Ivanka, Mirjana, Vicka, and the other Ivan, became known as the six Medjugorje visionaries. It was on this day that the children first spoke with Our Lady. That's why the anniversary is celebrated on June 25, the day the group was formed by Our Lady.

tears and very excited and filled with emotion, we said to those grown-ups who were seated around the table, "We saw Our Lady!" But I remember well that the apples that were on the table began to fly towards us and they said, "Do not ever say anything like that! You must not make jokes about that." And they chased us out and we each went home to our own homes.

When I came home, I said to my grandmother, "Grandmother, I have seen Our Lady." She said to me, "My child, this is not possible. Someone must be on the hillside tending to their sheep." Because at that time I had never heard of anything like this. I had never heard of Fatima or Lourdes and the possibility of Our Lady appearing on earth. That night was the longest night of my life. I kept asking myself, "Is this truly possible?" Because whenever we said something to the grown-ups, they all told us, this is not possible.

So the second day, already word had spread through villages nearby and some other people were coming to see what was happening. And the six of us visionaries, we gathered at the spot and I remember that my grandmother was there holding my hand and saying, "Whatever is there, you will not go." But three times a great light shined and we were drawn with such power up the hill, no one was able to stop us.

When we came before Our Lady, there are no words to describe the feeling that I felt—such *beauty;* such *grace* and feeling of motherly blessing came from her. I have no words to describe that feeling. My eyes had never seen such beauty; I could not imagine such a beautiful thing would exist. To describe her, my words, my vocabulary is too poor. But I can tell you that she wears a gray gown, a white veil, and a crown of stars. She has dark hair, blue eyes, and floats on a cloud. At that moment, I immediately knew that she was the Mother of God and I asked her, "Our Lady, where is my mother?" because my mother had died two months before that day. She smiled and she told me, "Your mother is with me." She told us, "Do not be afraid of anything. I will always be with you."

And those other people that had gathered could see that something unusual was happening to the six of us. When we went back to that spot again, on the third day, some of the parents advised us to take Holy Water to sprinkle the apparition. When Our Lady came, Vicka stood up and she sprinkled her with holy water. And Vicka said,

"If you are of God, stay with us. If you are not, go away." Then Our Lady smiled and she said, "I am the Queen of Peace." And her first message to us was "peace." After this she gave us the messages of calling us to peace, prayer, fasting, penance, and conversion. From the very first day until today, these are the most important messages from Medjugorje, because within these things there are simply all of our questions and all of our answers.

From 1981 until 1985, I did have regular apparitions every single day. And through those years Our Lady told me her life story. She also told me the future of the Church and the future of the world. And I wrote all of these things down. And when she tells me that it is the time, and when she tells me to whom I should give these writings, then it will become public knowledge. On the seventh of May in 1985, it was my last daily apparition from Our Lady. On that day, I received the tenth secret message and Our Lady told me that I will no longer see her every day, but once a year, on the twenty-fifth of June.

Since 1985 until the present day I do see her every year on June 25, and through this she has given me a great gift and also a great gift to the whole world. Because every person asks themselves, "Does life after death truly exist?" And I stand here today as a living witness to the fact that it does indeed exist. On that day, on my final daily apparition, I was able to see my mother and she told me, "My child, I am so proud of you."

Our Lady is showing us the way. It is up to us whether we will accept it, but she invites us every day, "Dear Children, open your hearts." In one of her messages she said, "Dear Children, if only you knew how much I love you, you would weep with joy." And so let us open up our hearts and open up our families and lives so that love and peace can enter them.

Of the six of us visionaries, each one of us has a specific mission. Our Lady has chosen me to pray especially for families. She wishes that prayer in the family is renewed, that we go to Mass on Sunday, that we go to confession once every month, and that the Bible is in the center of our lives and the center of our families. In the very beginning she was asking us to pray seven Our Fathers, Hail Marys, and Glory Be's every day, and after this, every year we received a greater and greater homework from her—to pray the rosary, and then to pray two rosaries, and now to pray all three. She has also invited us to fast on bread and water Wednesdays and Fridays. Many people say this is so difficult to do, but she tells us anything that is done with love and with your heart is no longer difficult.

Every day I pray for all of the families in this world, and in the same way I ask those families to pray for my family. I thank you for wanting to hear Our Lady's messages, and I thank even more those who wish to live her messages in their life.

On twenty-fifth of every month Our Lady gives a message to the entire world. So, on November 25, 2008, this was her most recent message to all of us:

> *"Dear Children, today also, I am calling you, in this time of grace, to pray for little Jesus to be born in your heart. May He, who is peace itself, give peace to the entire world through you. Therefore, little children, pray without ceasing for this turbulent world without hope, so that you may become witnesses of peace for all. May hope begin to flow through your hearts as a river of grace. Thank you for having responded to my call."*

And she [Ivanka] thanks everyone for coming and wishes you a most holy and blessed Christmas spent in peace and happiness, and maybe we can take one or two questions.

For the four years from 1981 to 1985, did the apparition always occur on the hill?

It was not always on the hill. No, the first week or so it was on the hill. But as the government police, who were communist at that time, they forbade the children to go on the hill or any gathering on the hill. The hill was covered with soldiers and dogs. So then they would meet in their family homes or in the fields, where the police could not find them, and then eventually it was in the chapel, and in the church, and then in the parish office with the priests. But it's not at all important where she [Ivanka] is or any of the visionaries at the time of the apparition; wherever they happen to be, there is a bright light three times and then Our Lady comes, or as Ivanka says it, "Everything else disappears—only *She* [Our Lady] is left.

Of the six visionaries, do they ever have a difference of opinion as to what they saw?

The six visionaries have always agreed on what they see and how she appears to them. There have been certain times when they have not *heard* the same exact words from her. If something was intended for some of them but not all of them, then even though the apparition was at that same moment, some heard some things, some heard other things, whatever was intended for them.

Does Ivanka experience any other earthly senses besides sight when she sees Our Lady, such as smell?

When Ivanka sees Our Lady, she sees her exactly as she sees you right now. But she does not experience her with any other earthly senses.

What is Medjugorje like now? Is it as holy as it was in the beginning?

Ivanka says that she believes that it is. If it has changed in any way, it has become *more* holy.

You said there's a message every month on the twenty-fifth. How do you get that message? How does it come to you?

Of the six visionaries, Ivanka, Mirjana, and Jakov, those three only see Our Lady once a year on different dates. The other three, Ivan, Marija, and Vicka, they still see her every single day. And so one of those three, her name is Marija, she is the one that receives that message for the world on the twenty-fifth. Once she hears it from Our Lady, she, in the Croatian language, she gives it to the priests in the parish and then it is interpreted into all of the languages of the world, and then it is given out even on the computers or by word of mouth or on pieces of paper—every which way it's possible.

Ivanka would like to thank you once more for coming here tonight. She would like to tell you that she will be praying for all of you and hopes that you will all be praying for her. Let us together pray one Our Father, Hail Mary, and Glory Be, to thank God for this gathering tonight.